Hello Friend!

We are deeply appreciative of your choice to incorporate our cozy coloring books into your tranquil moments.

It's an honor to contribute to your snug and serene retreats.

To further enhance our shared journey of relaxation and tranquility, we invite you to subscribe to our newsletter at

www.CozyColoringCorner.com

Imagine it as a soft reminder to indulge in some well-earned downtime, offering you the latest updates on our newest comforting editions and exclusive perks for our subscribers.

Our heartfelt thanks for allowing us to add a touch of coziness to your personal time.

Warmly,
The Cozy Coloring Crew

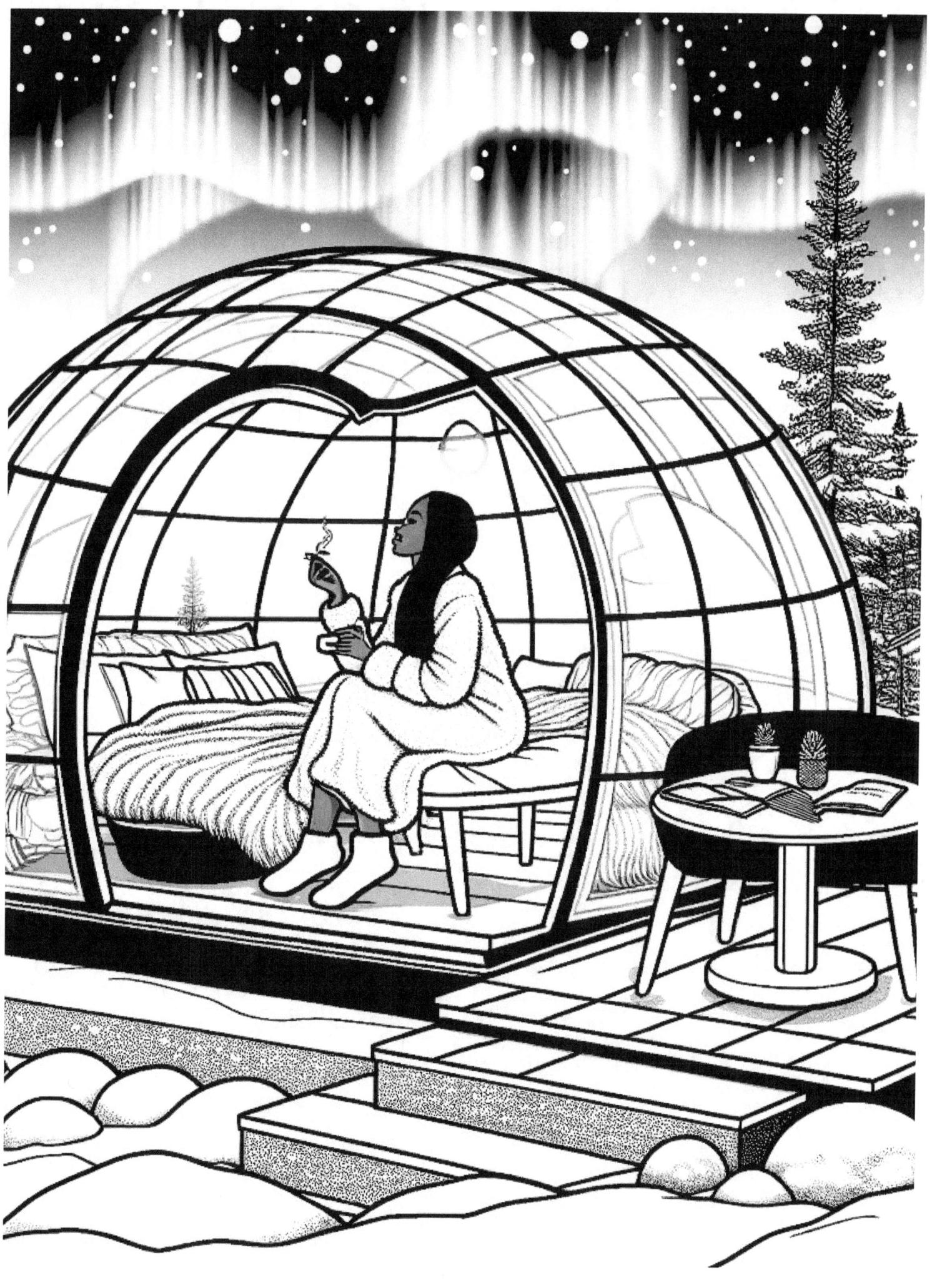

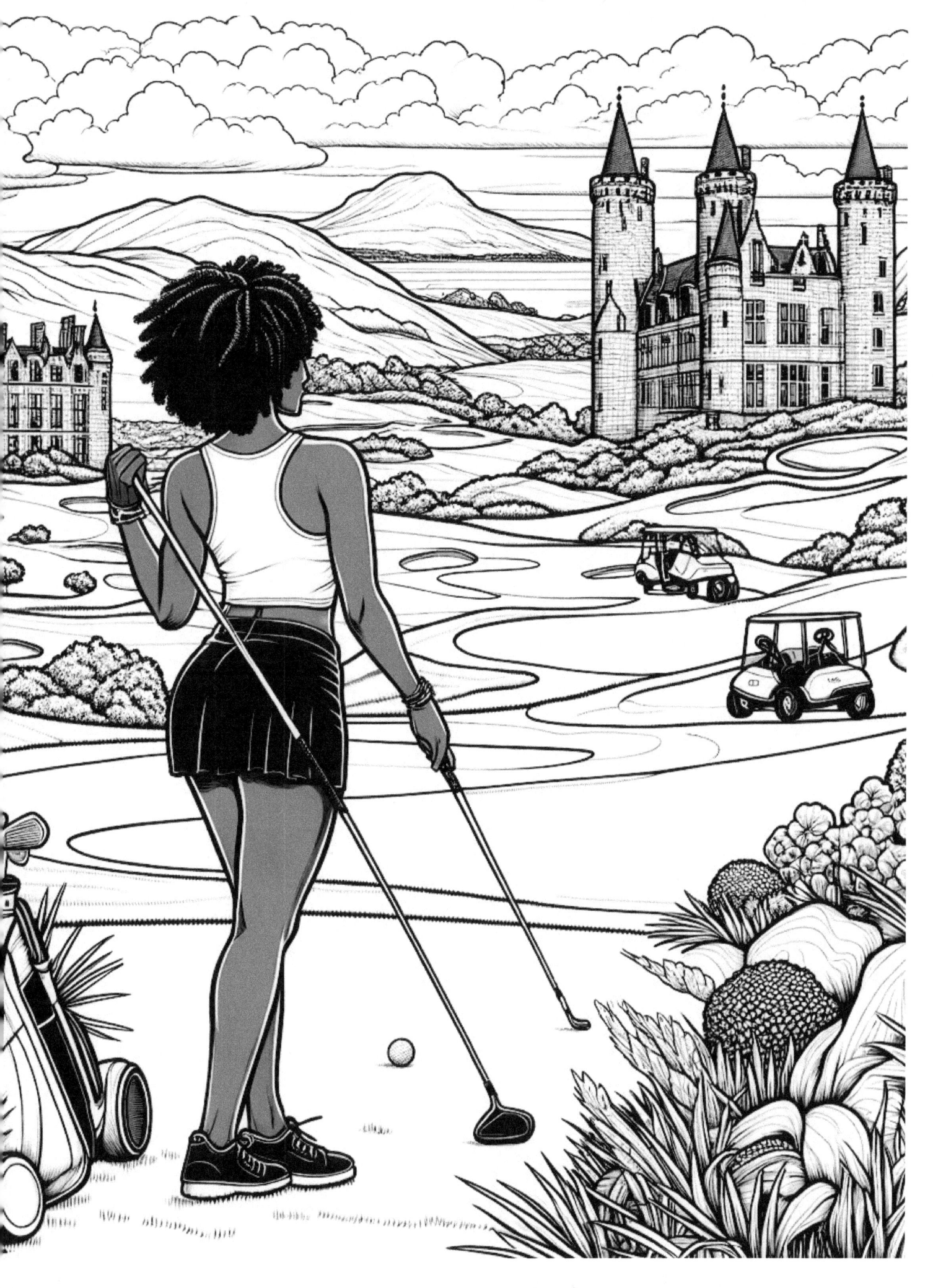

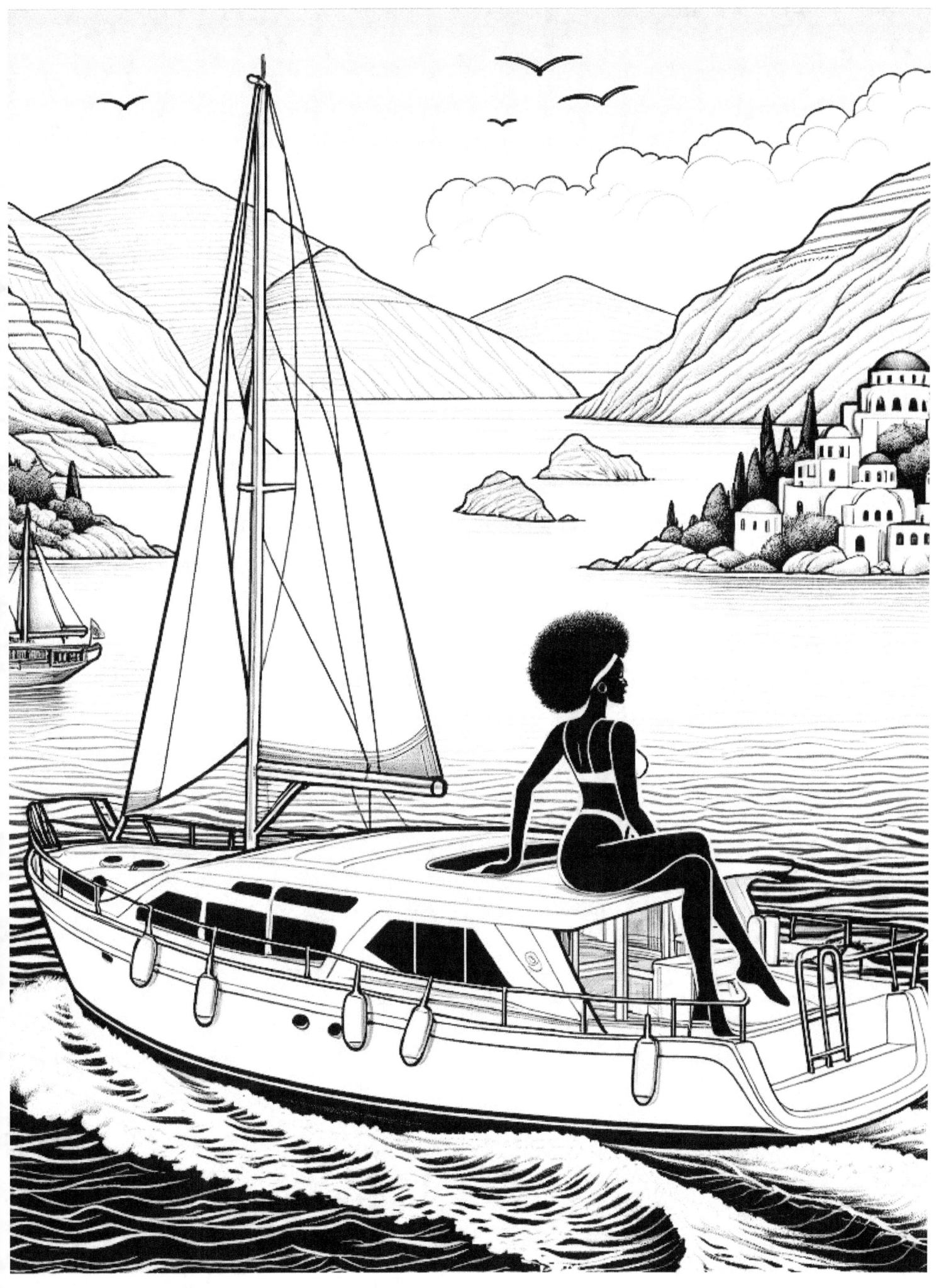

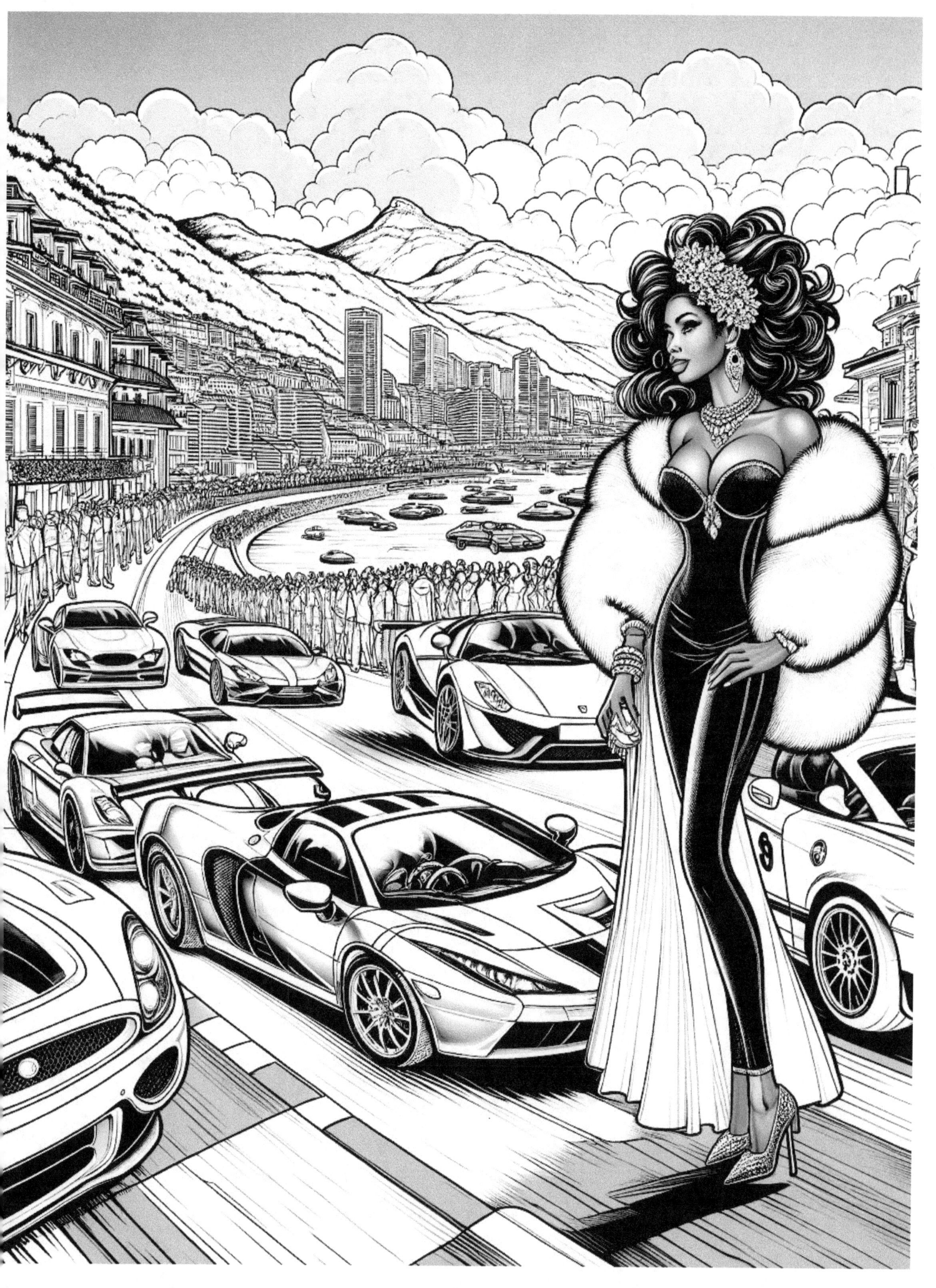

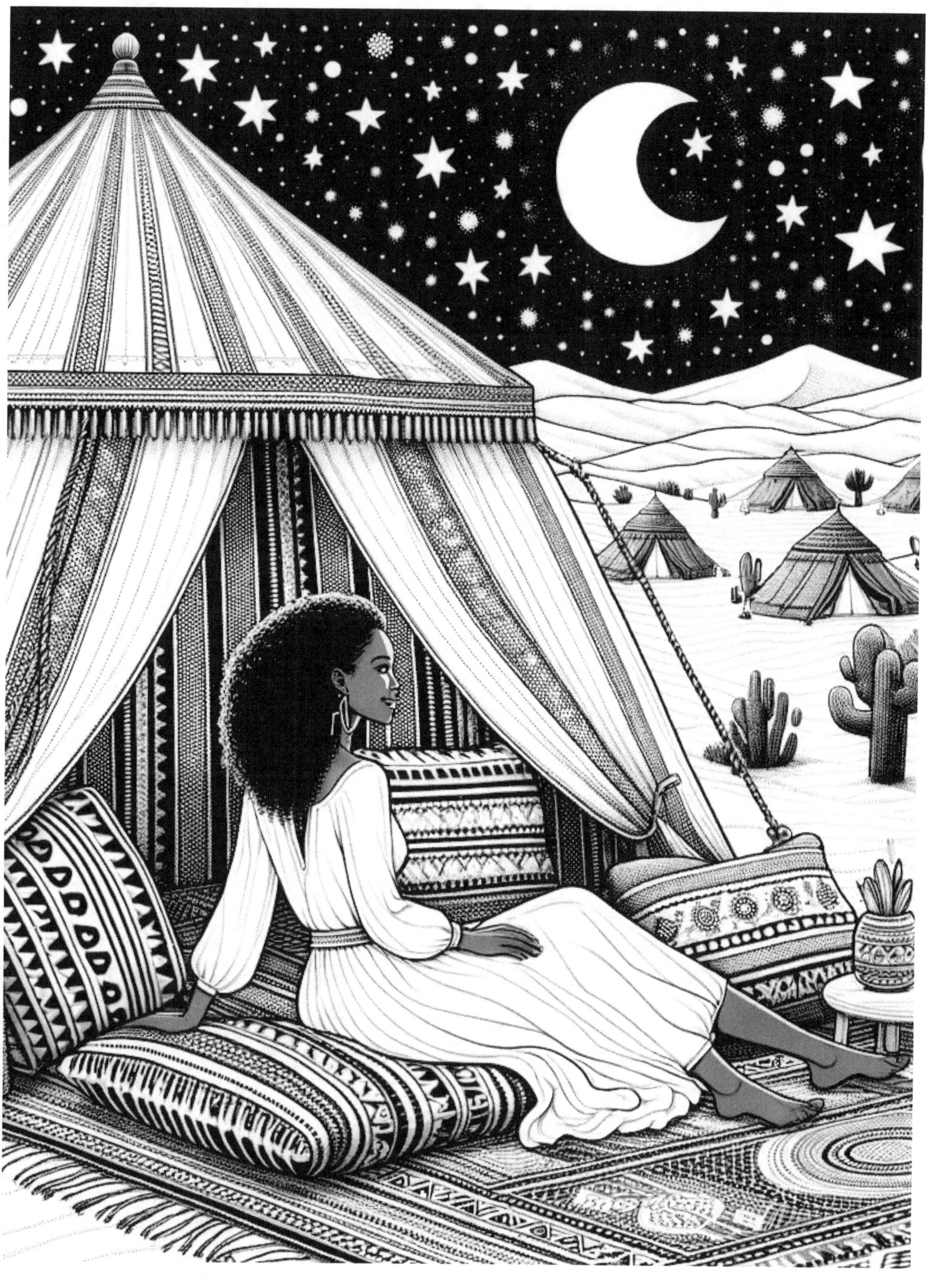

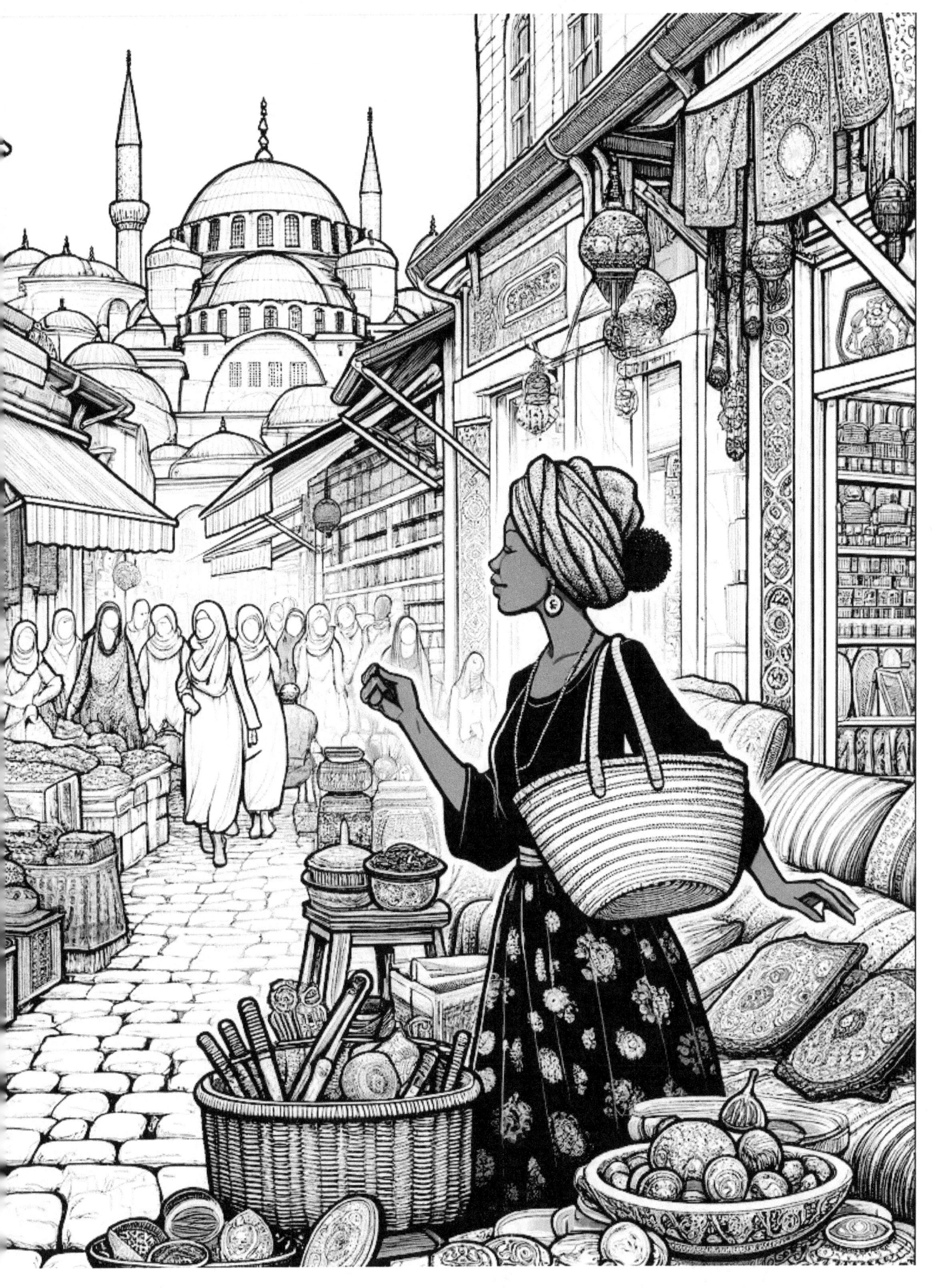

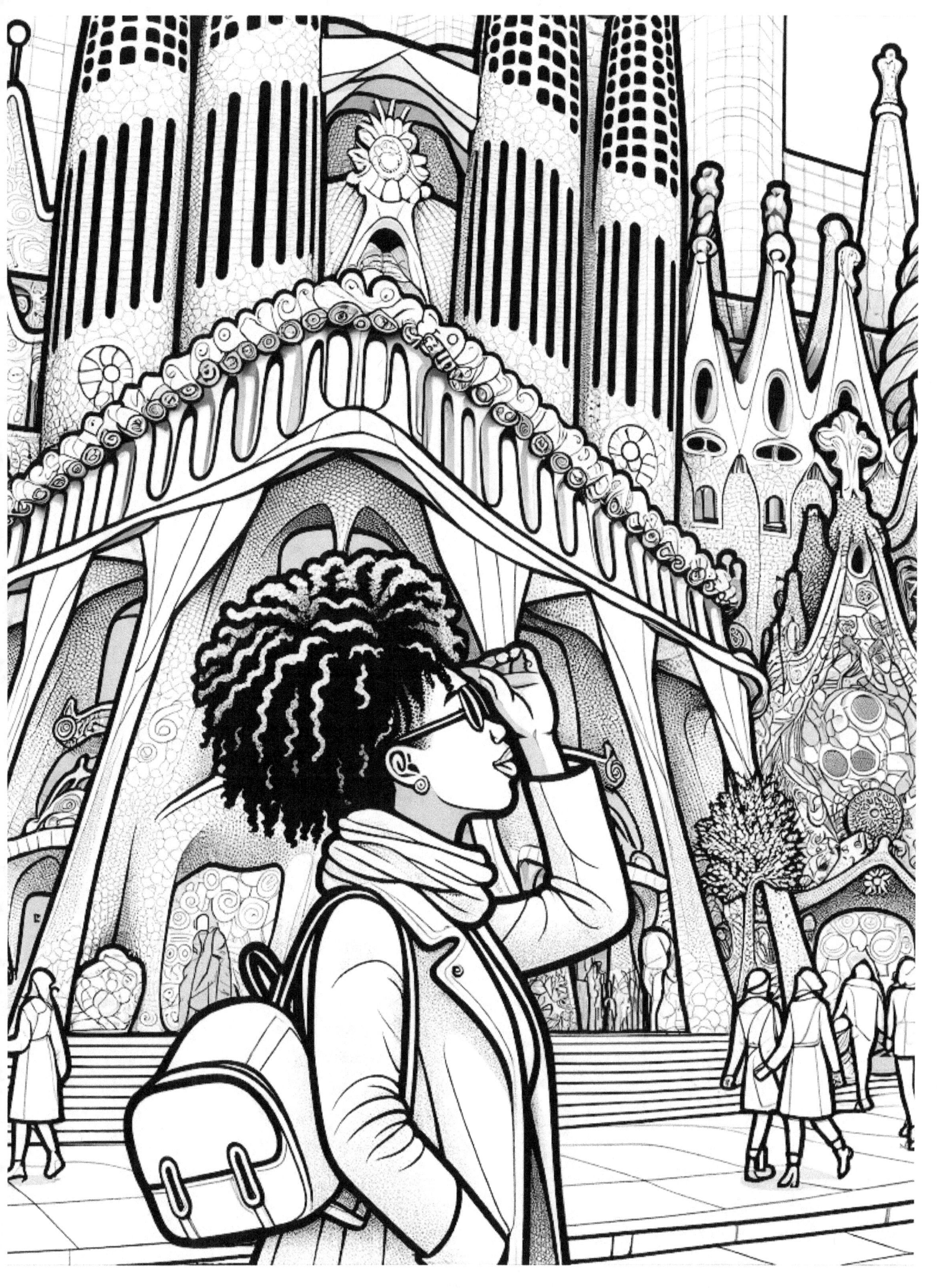

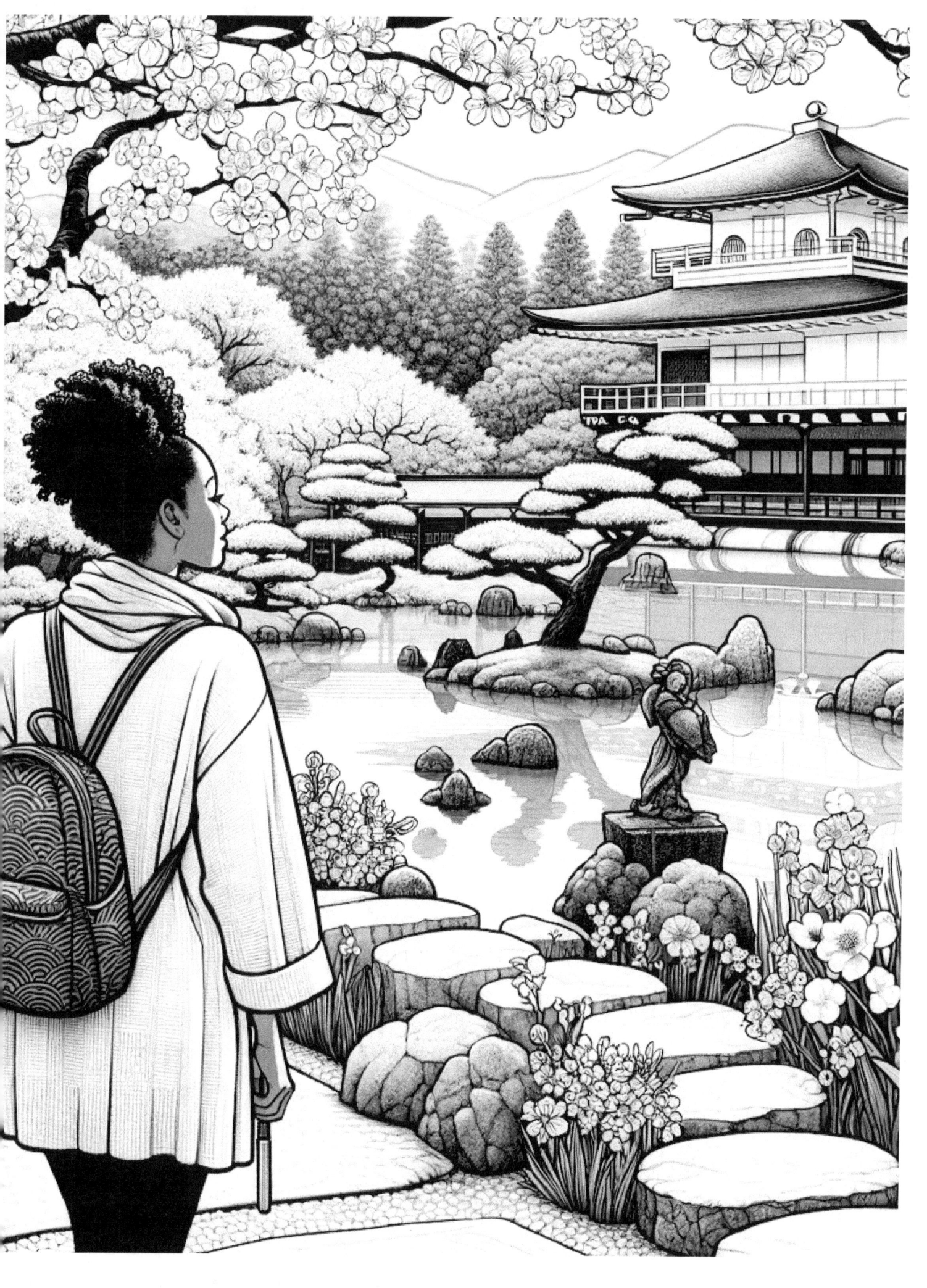

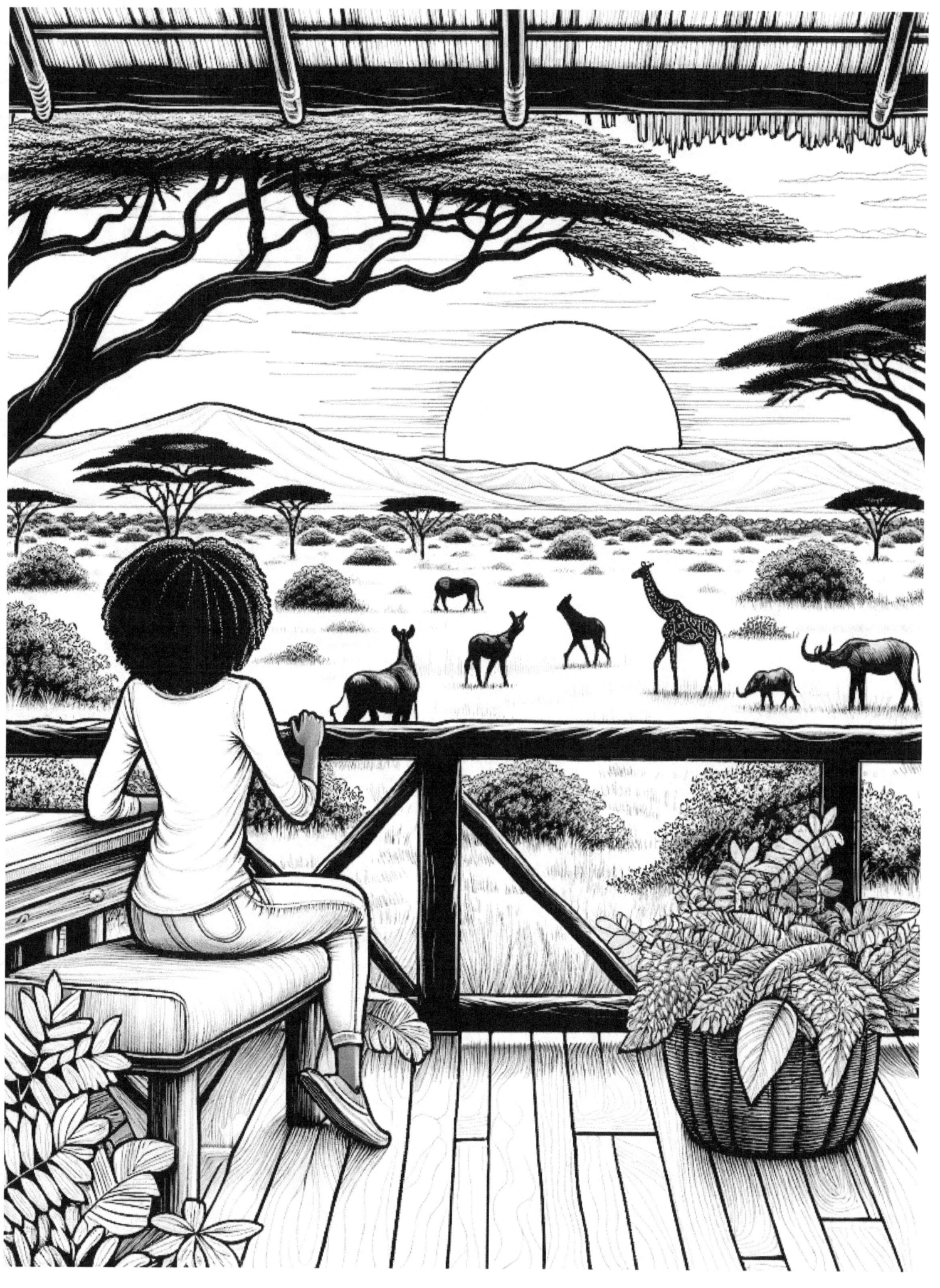

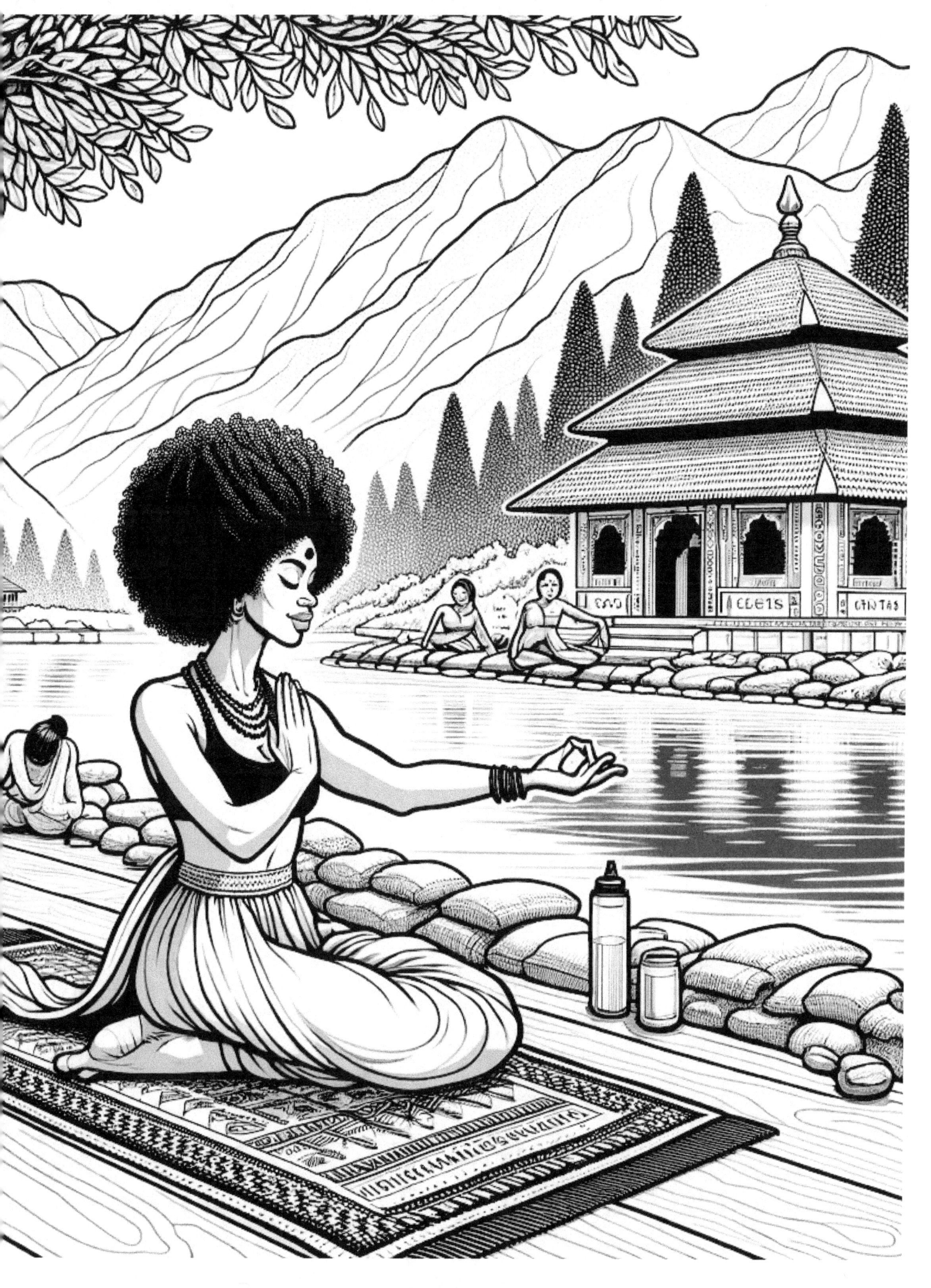

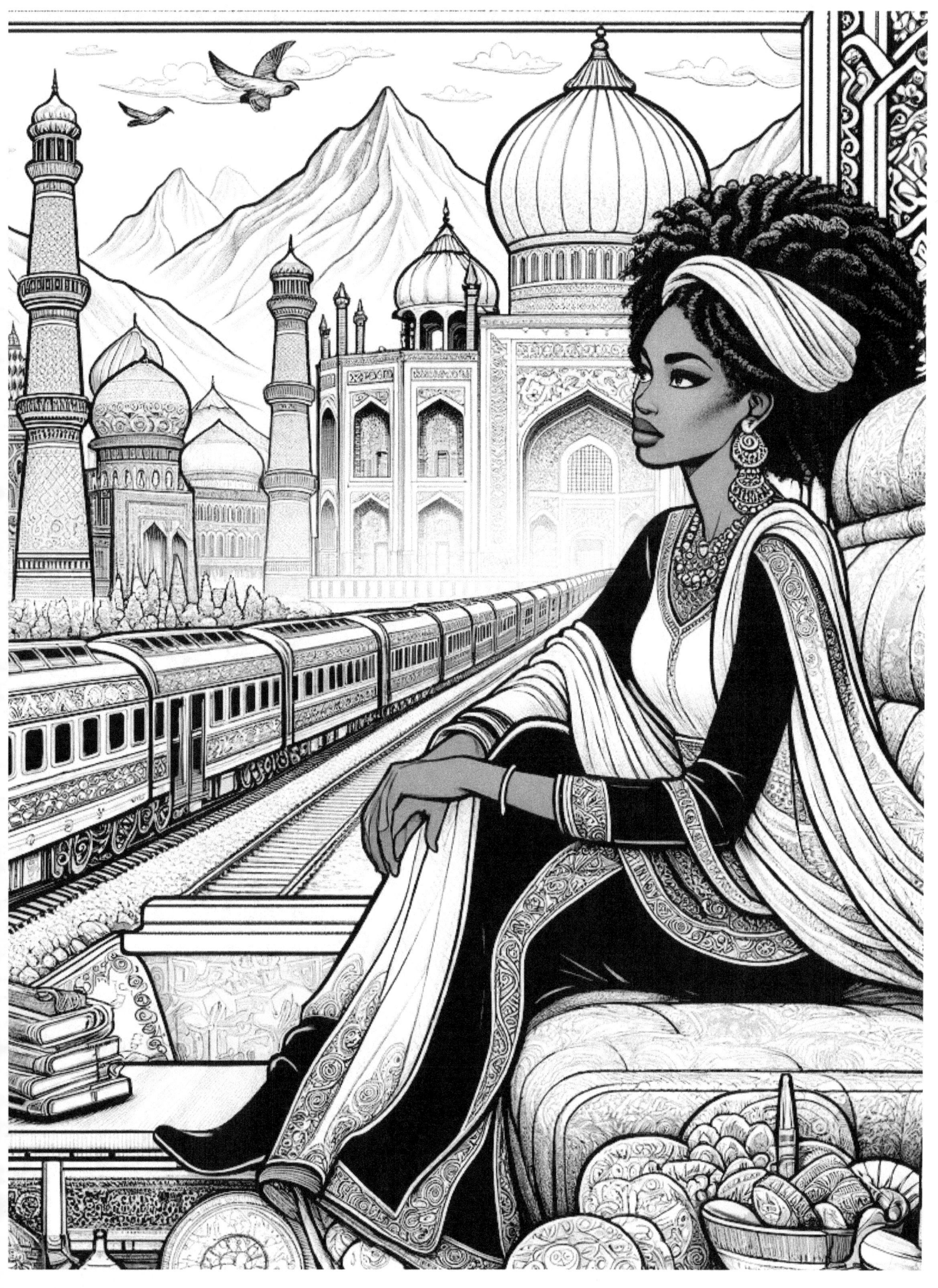

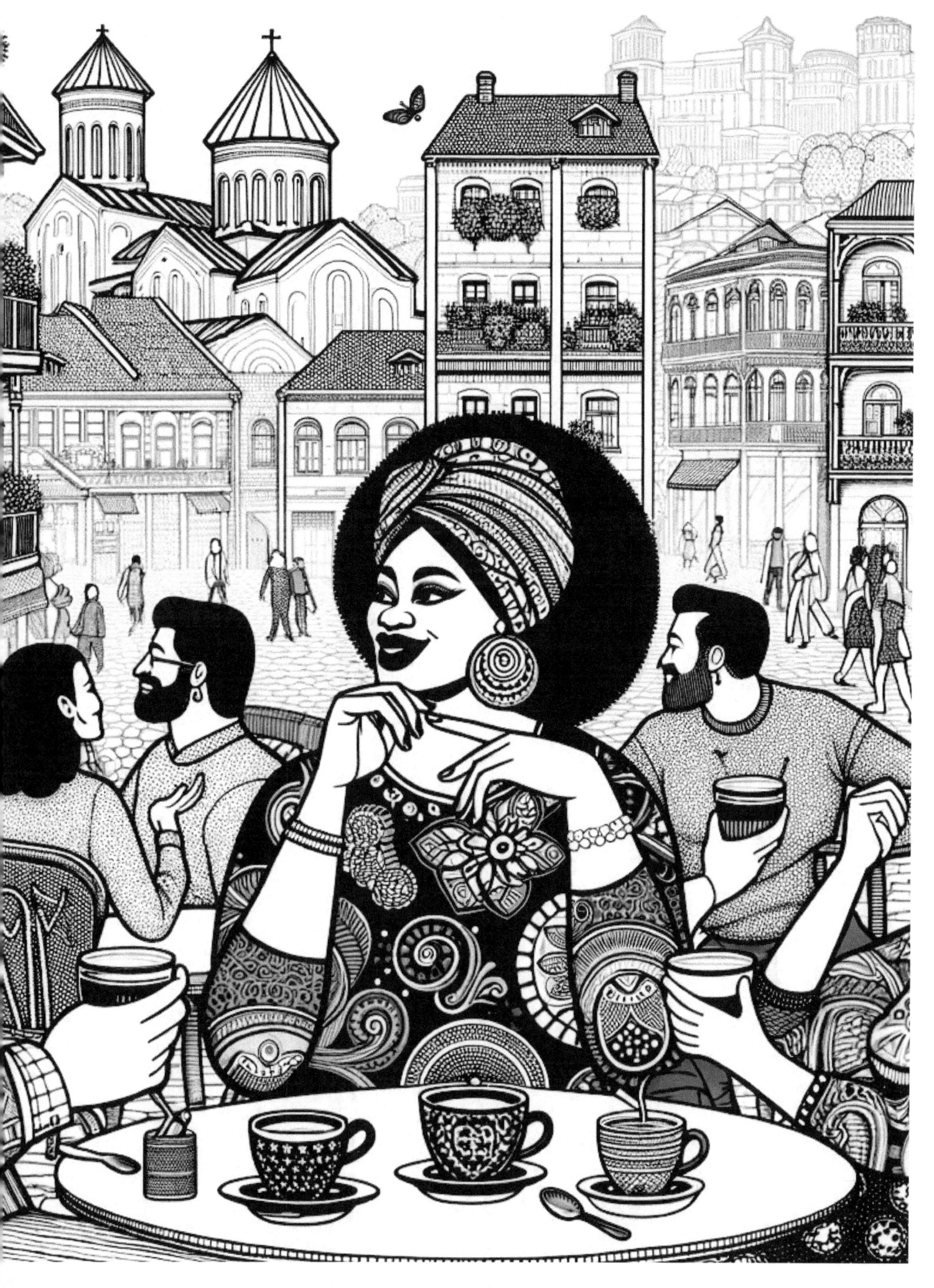

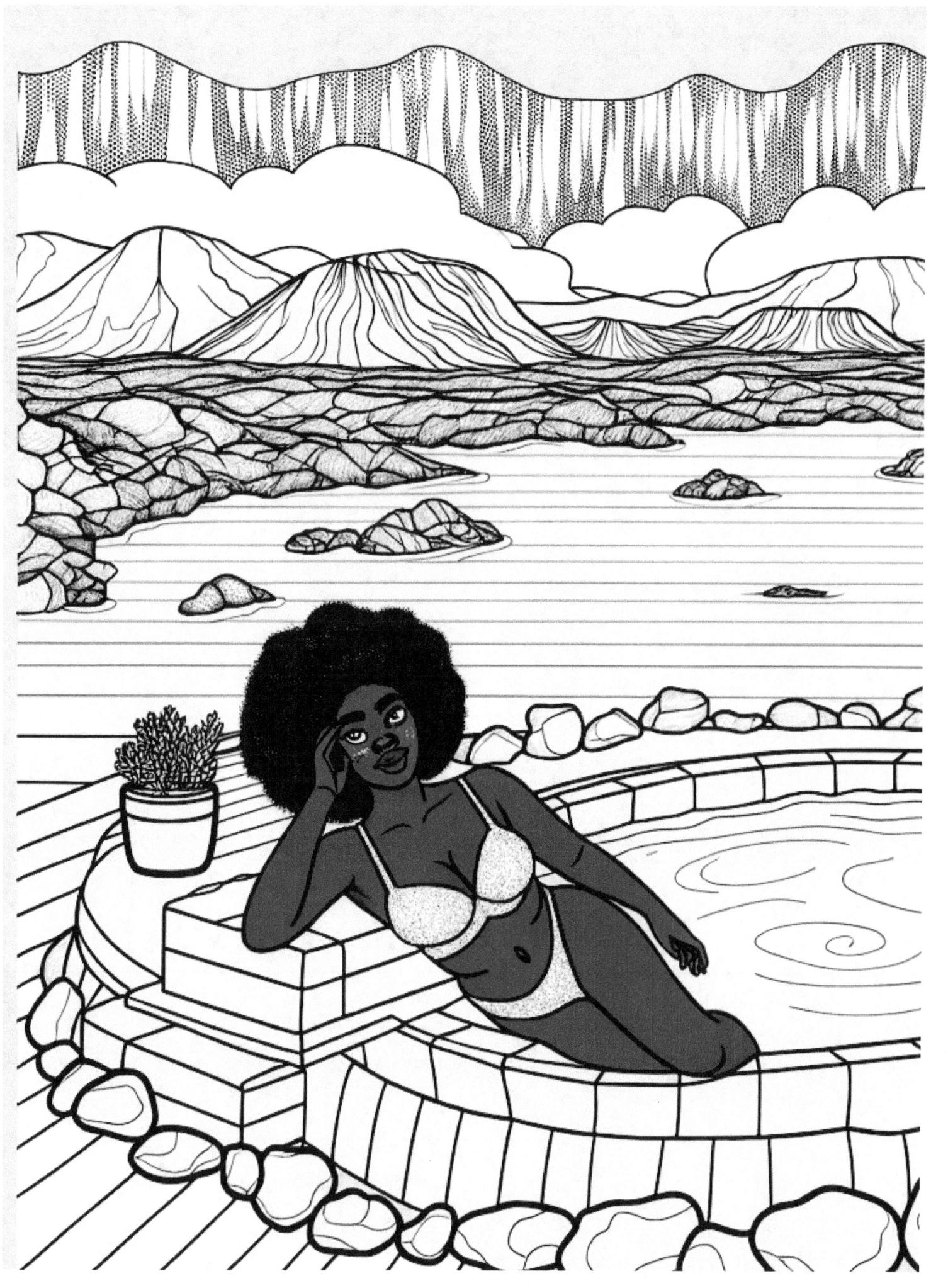

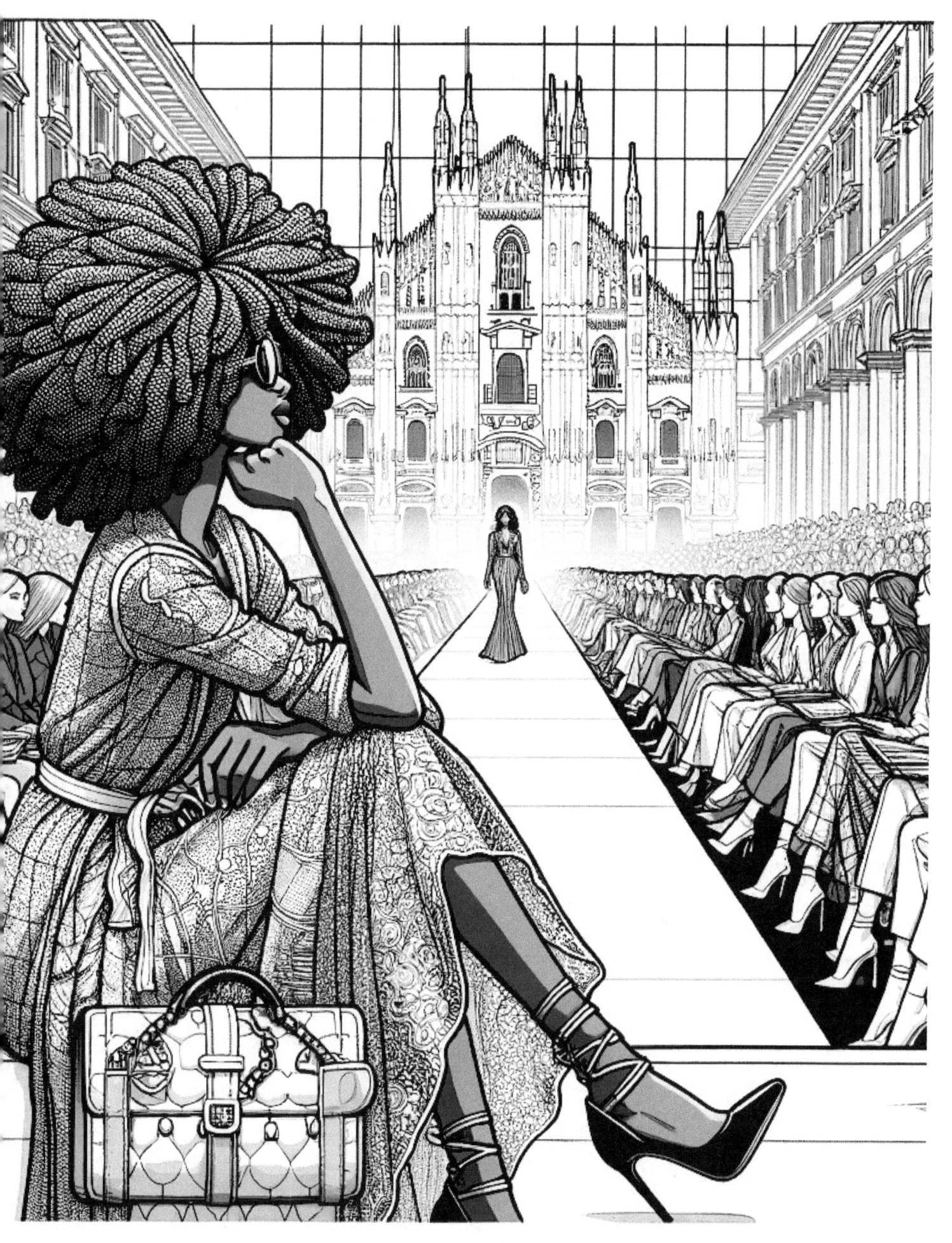

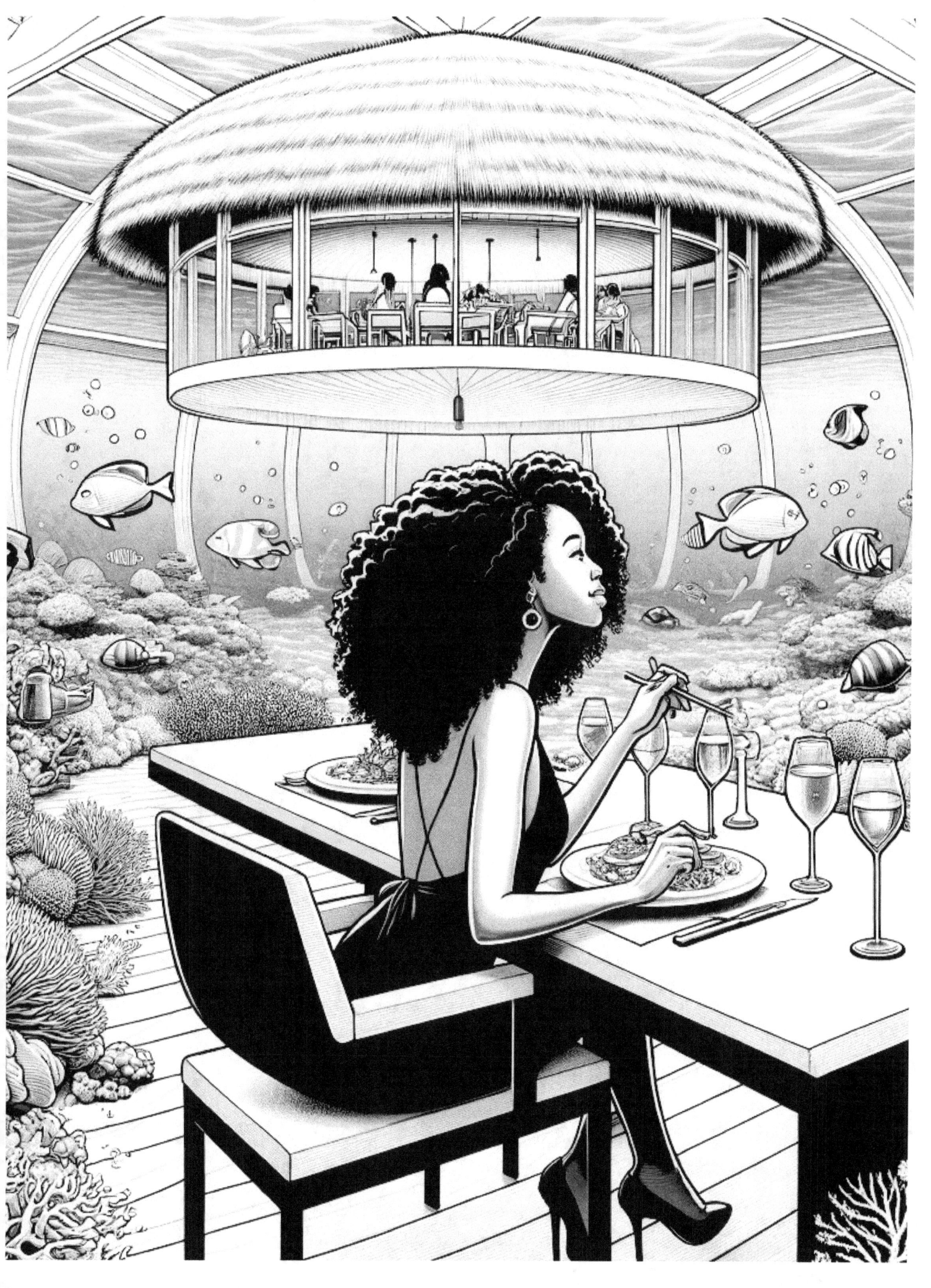

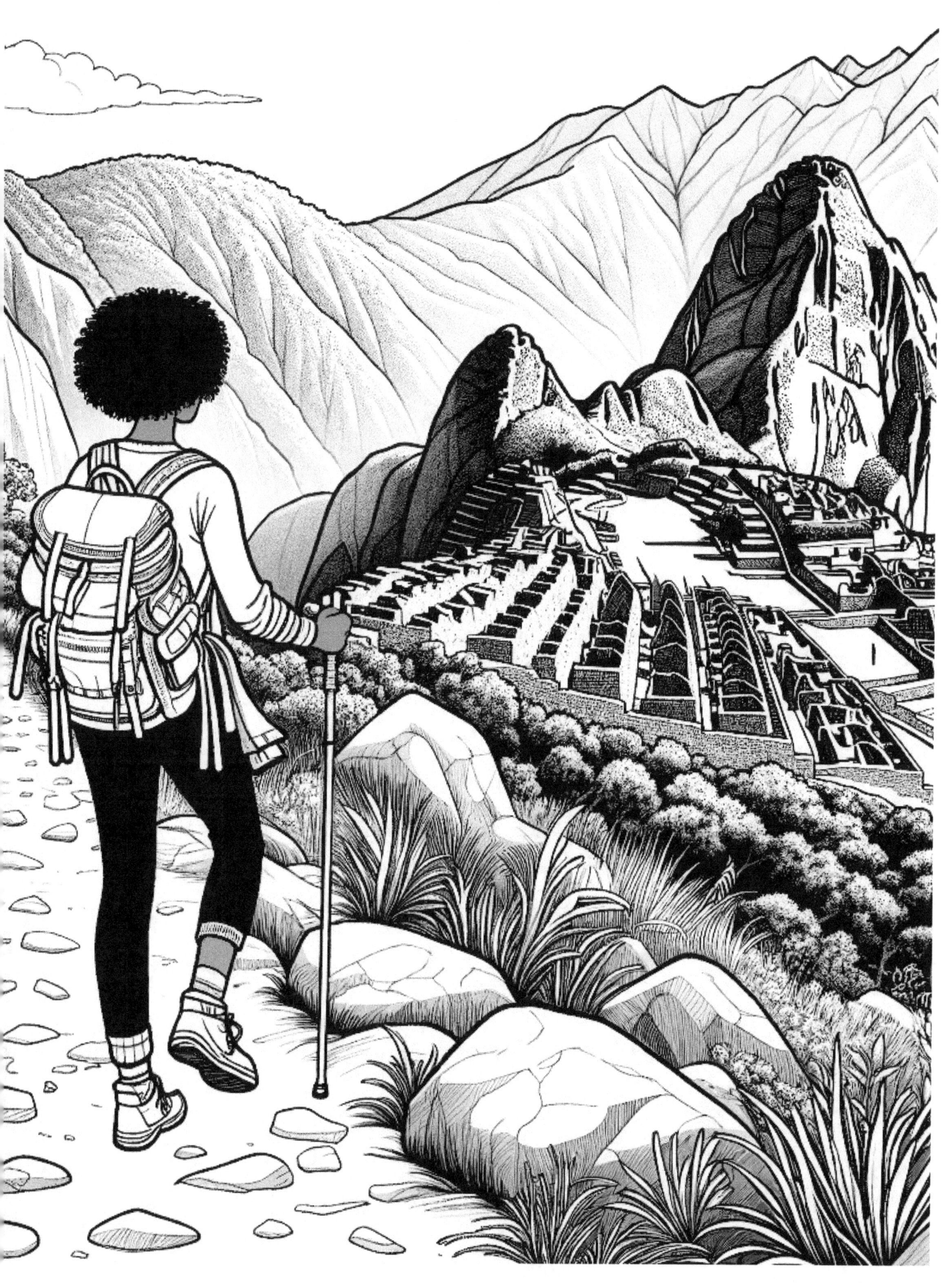

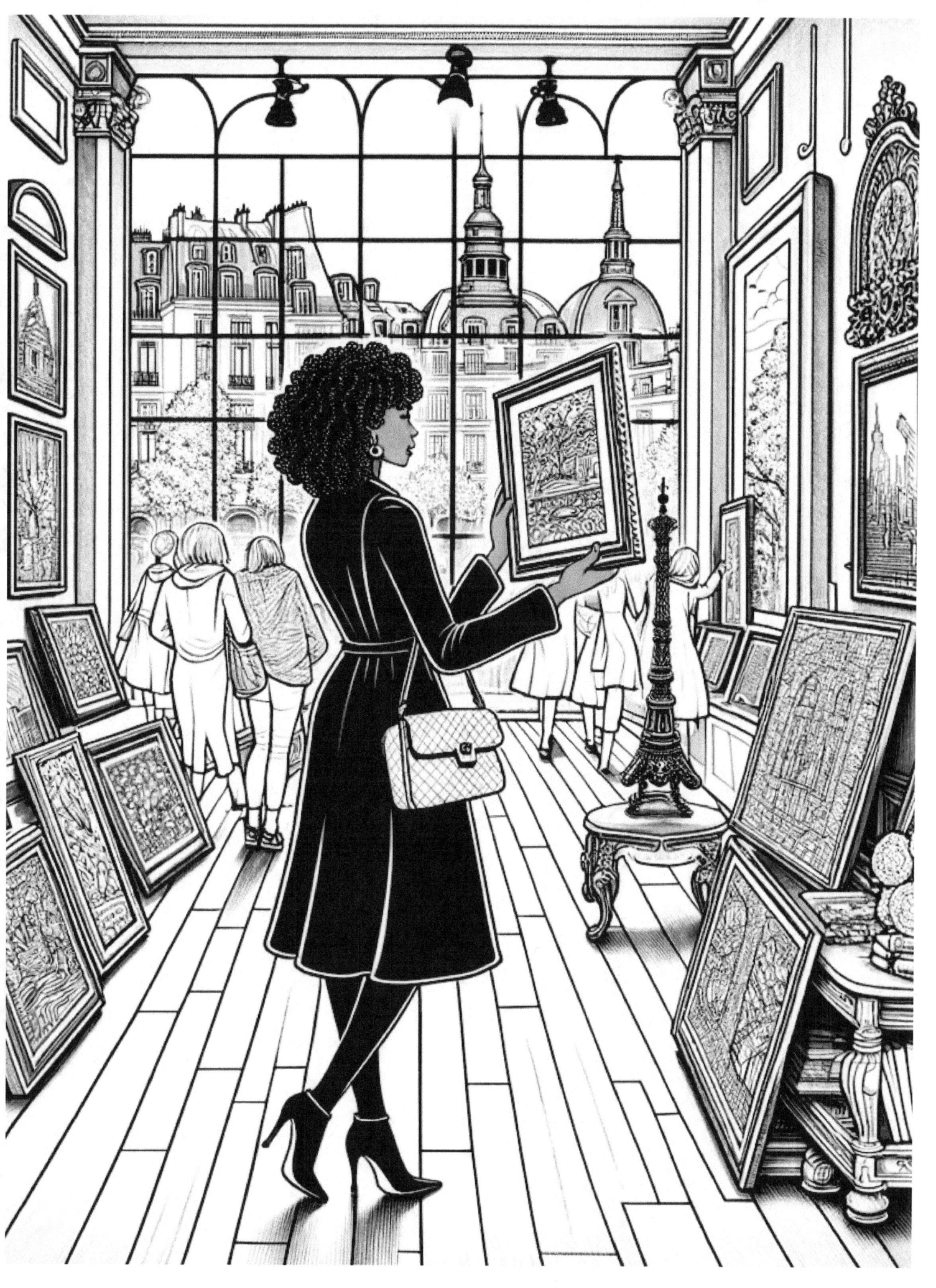

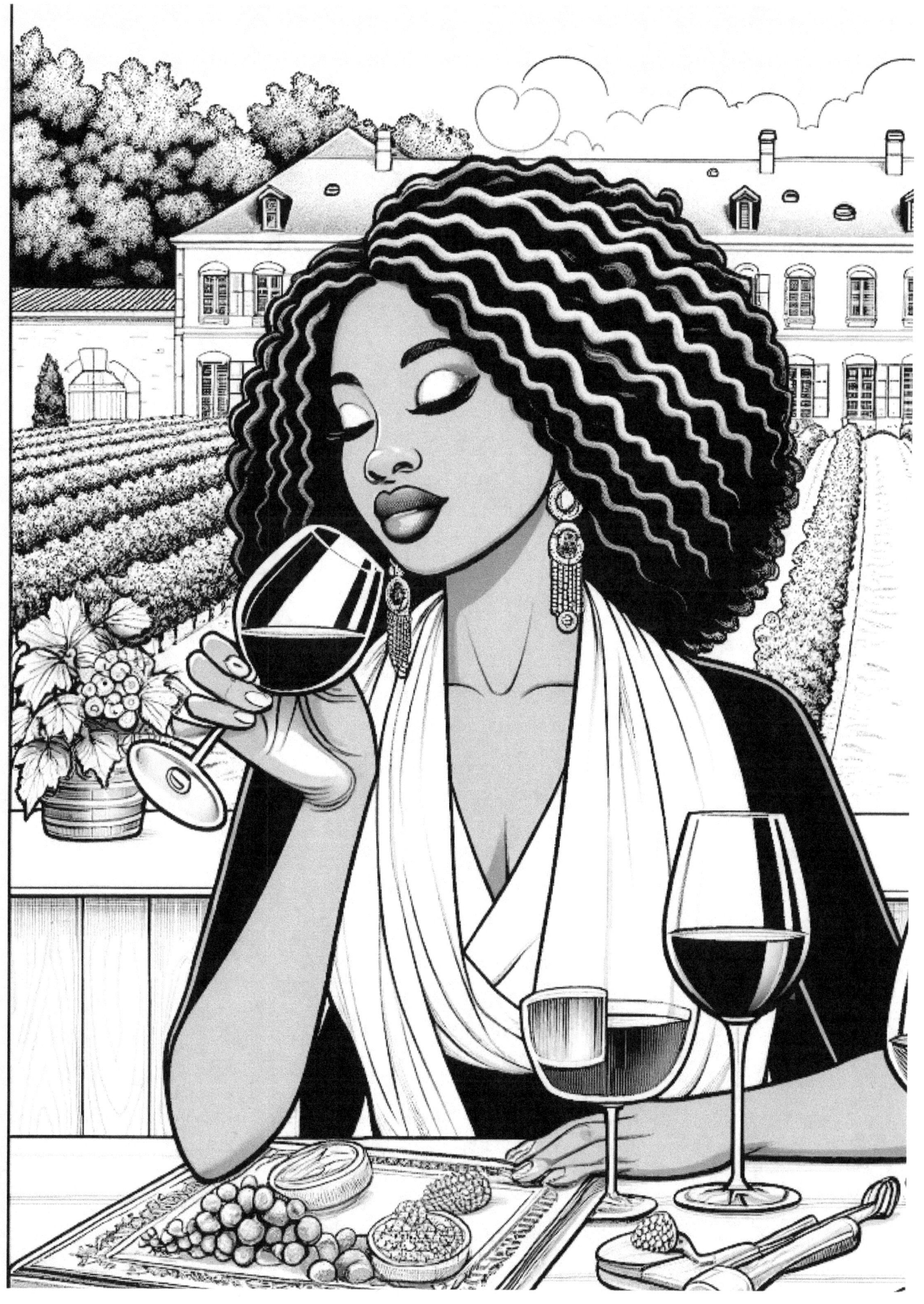

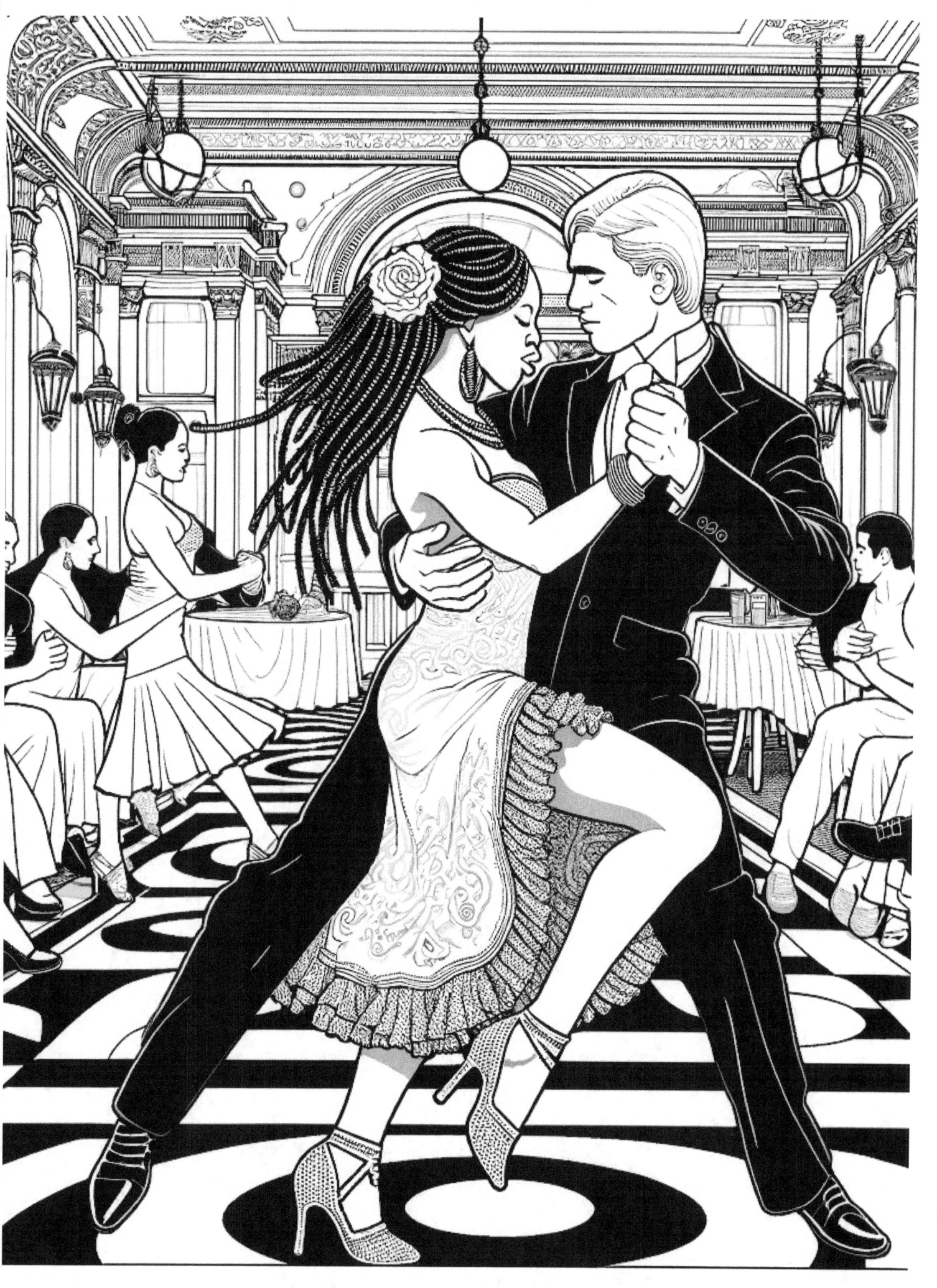

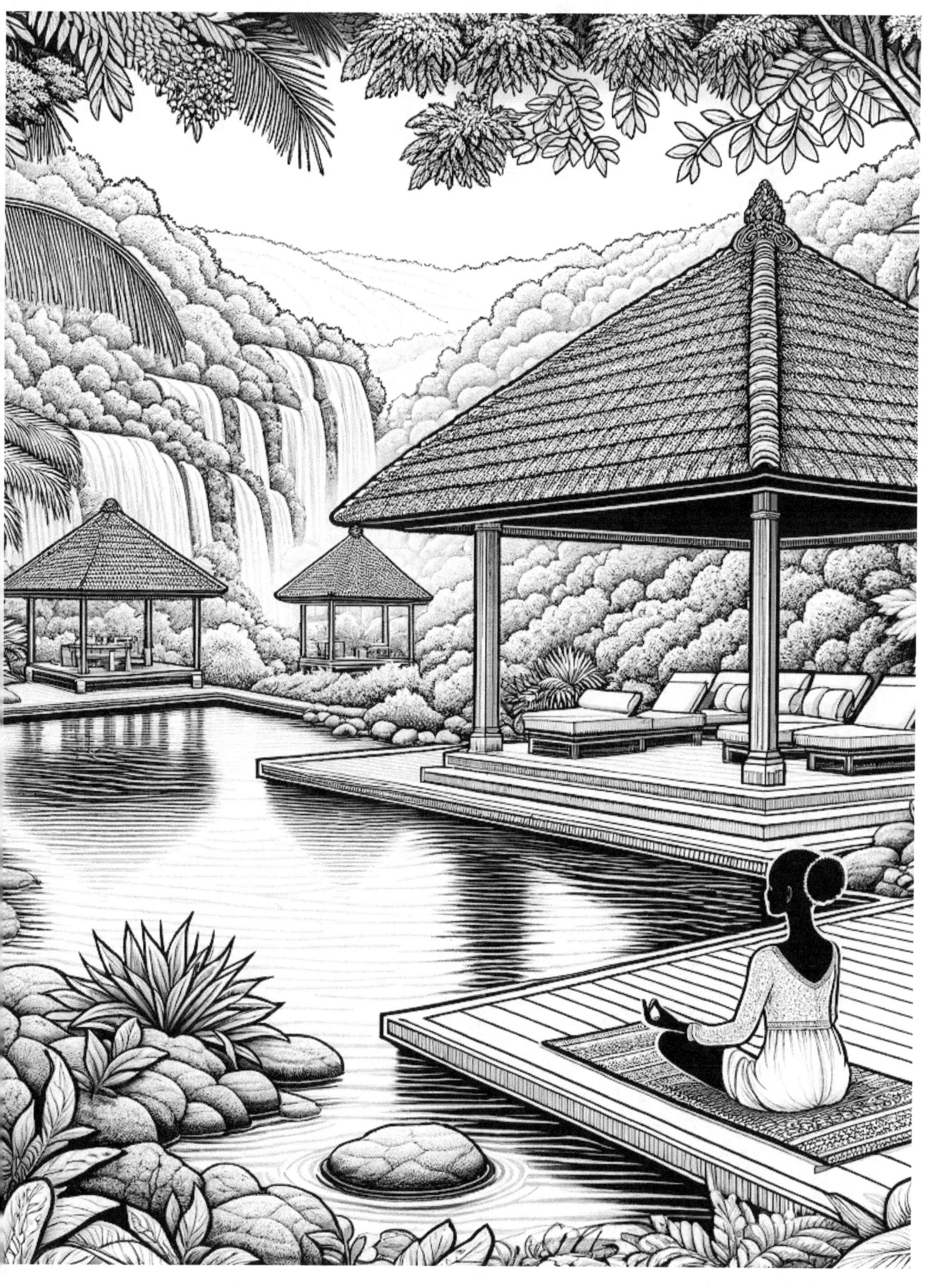

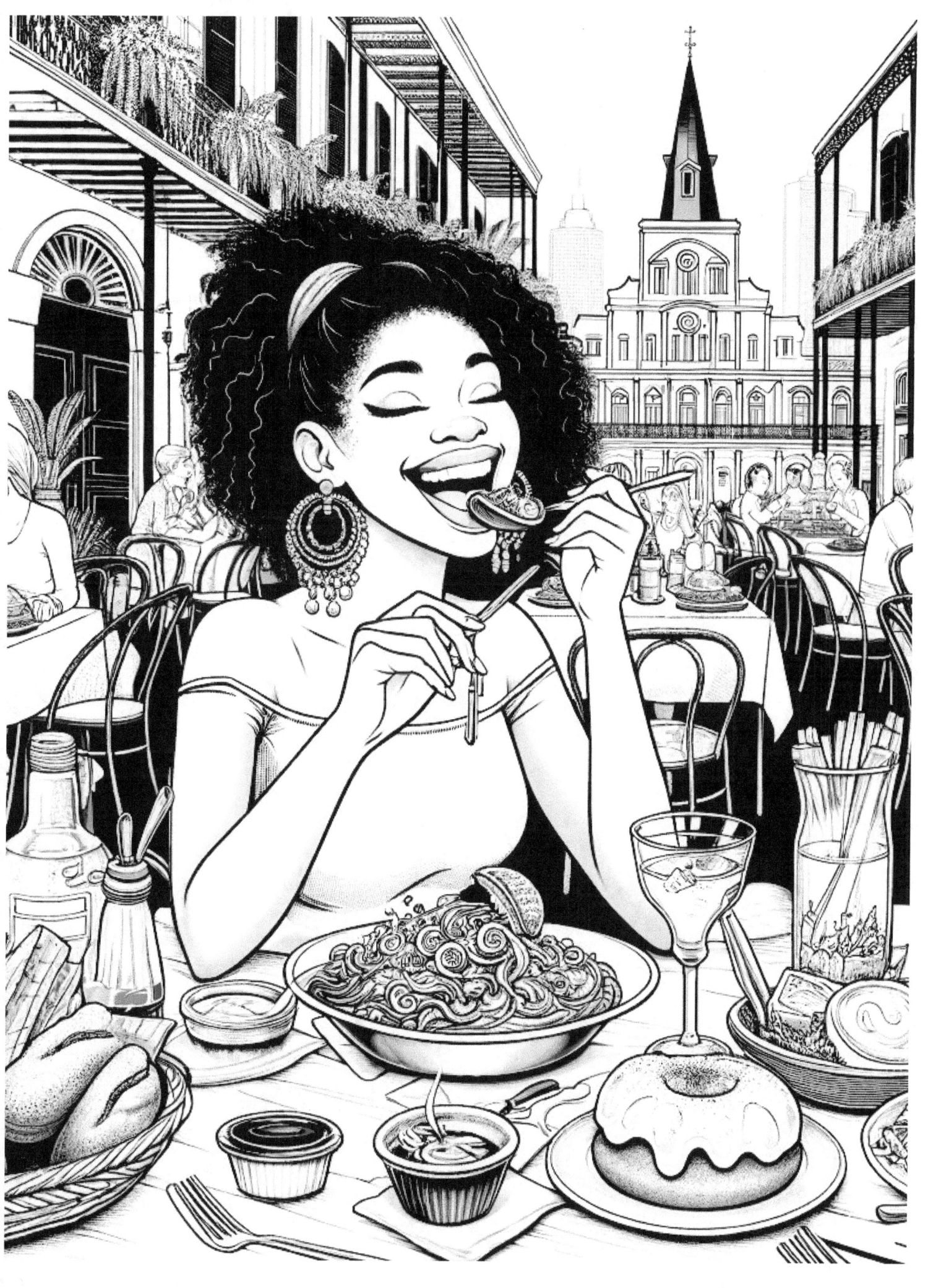

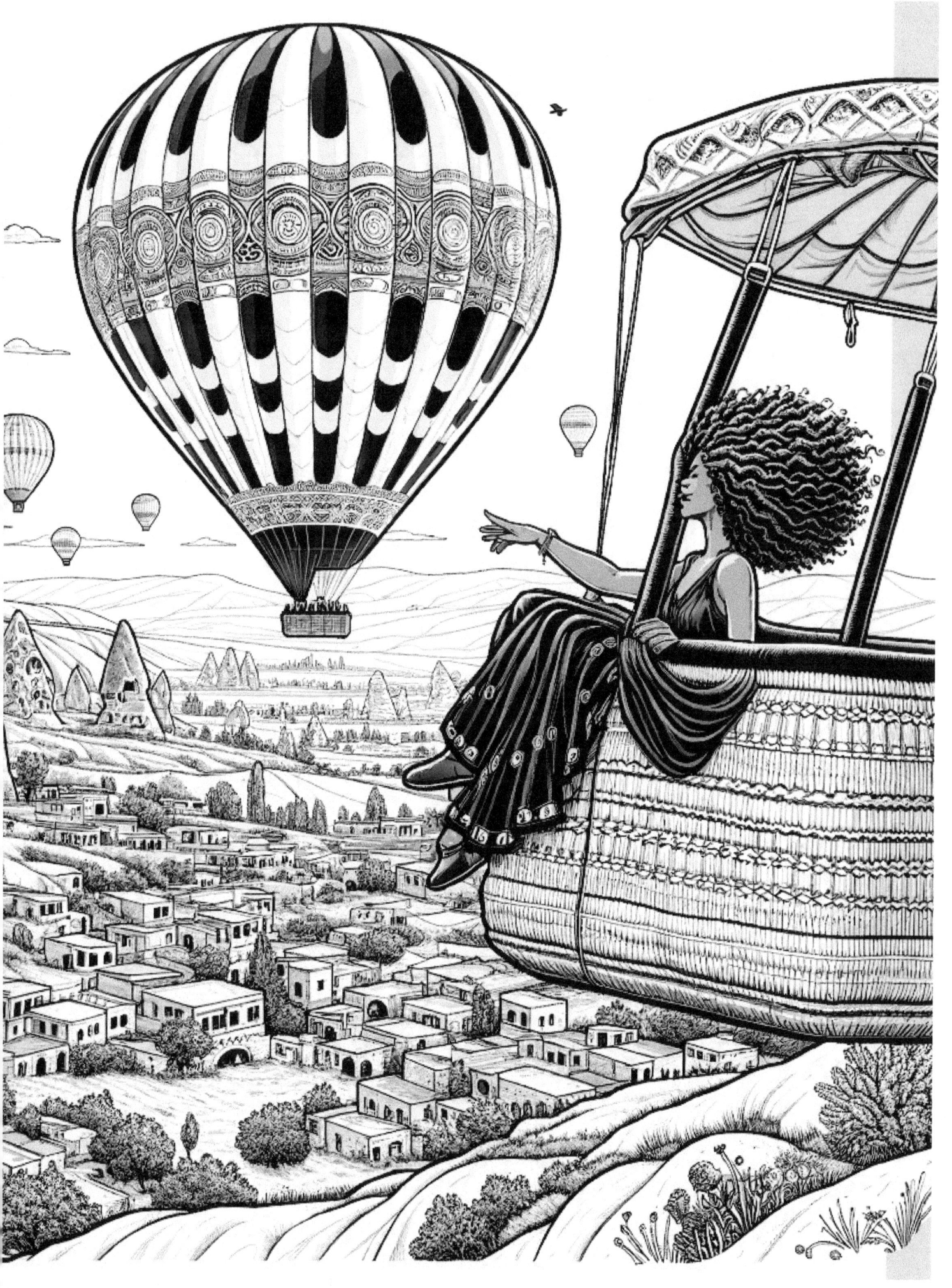

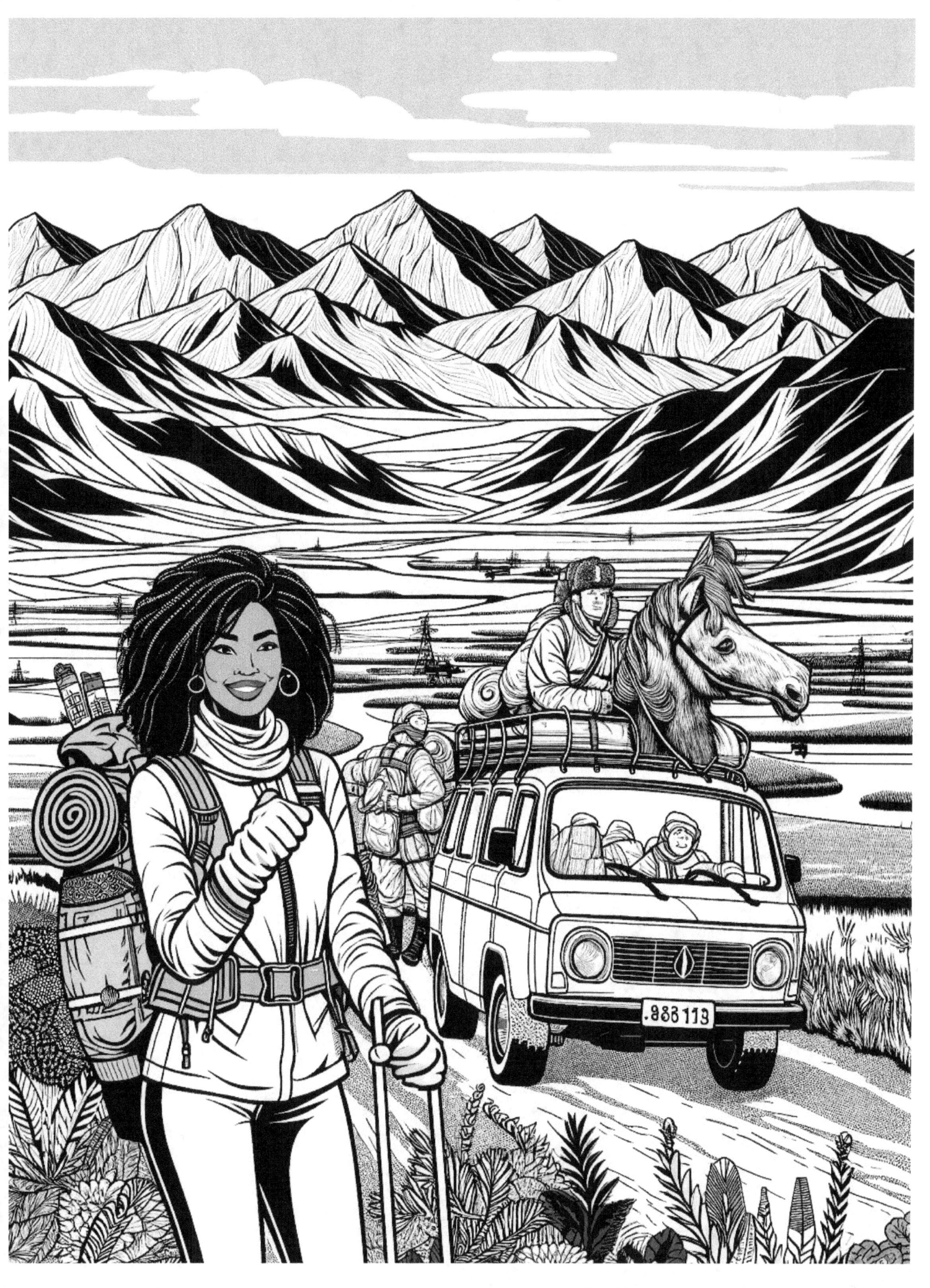

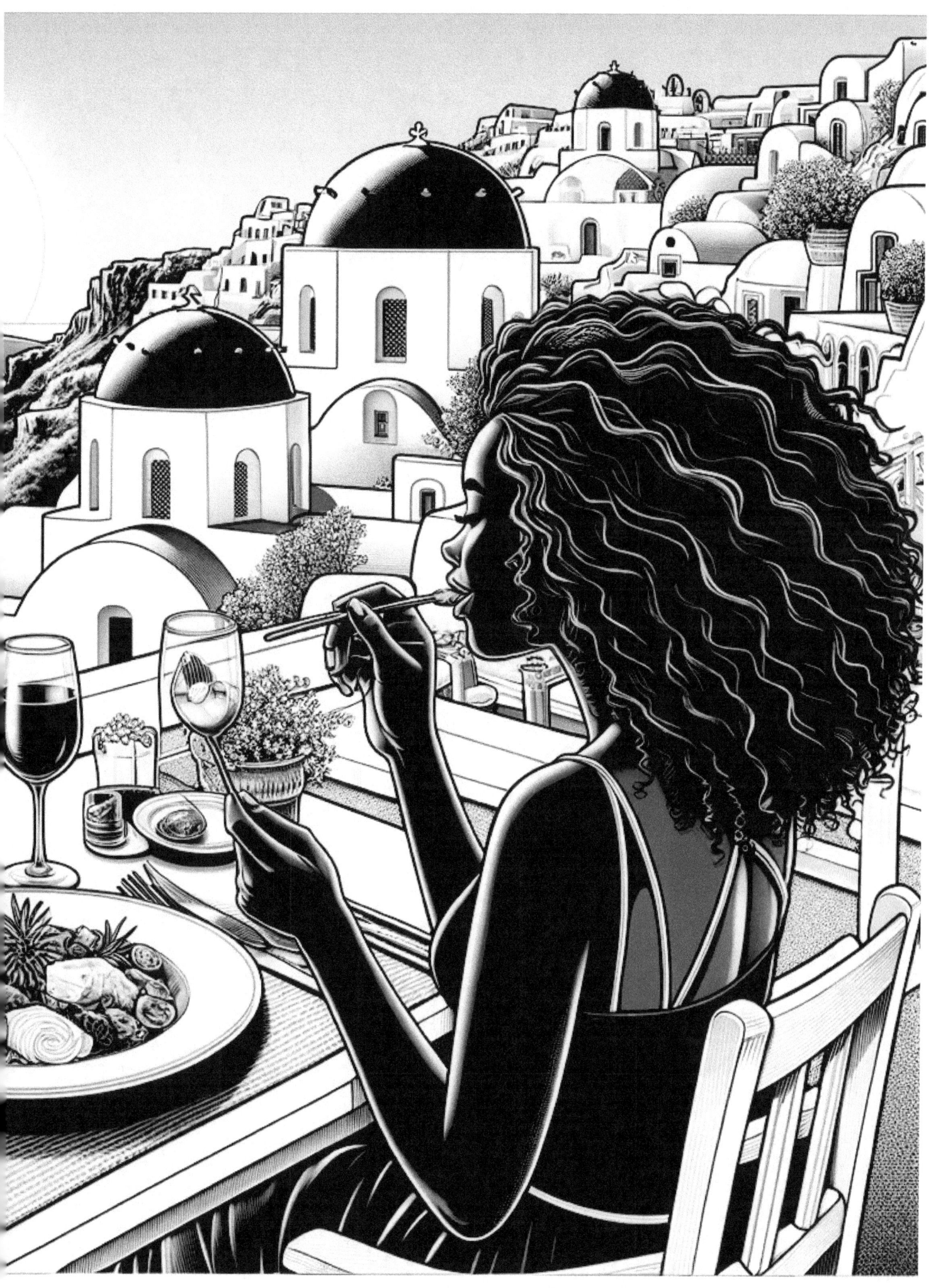

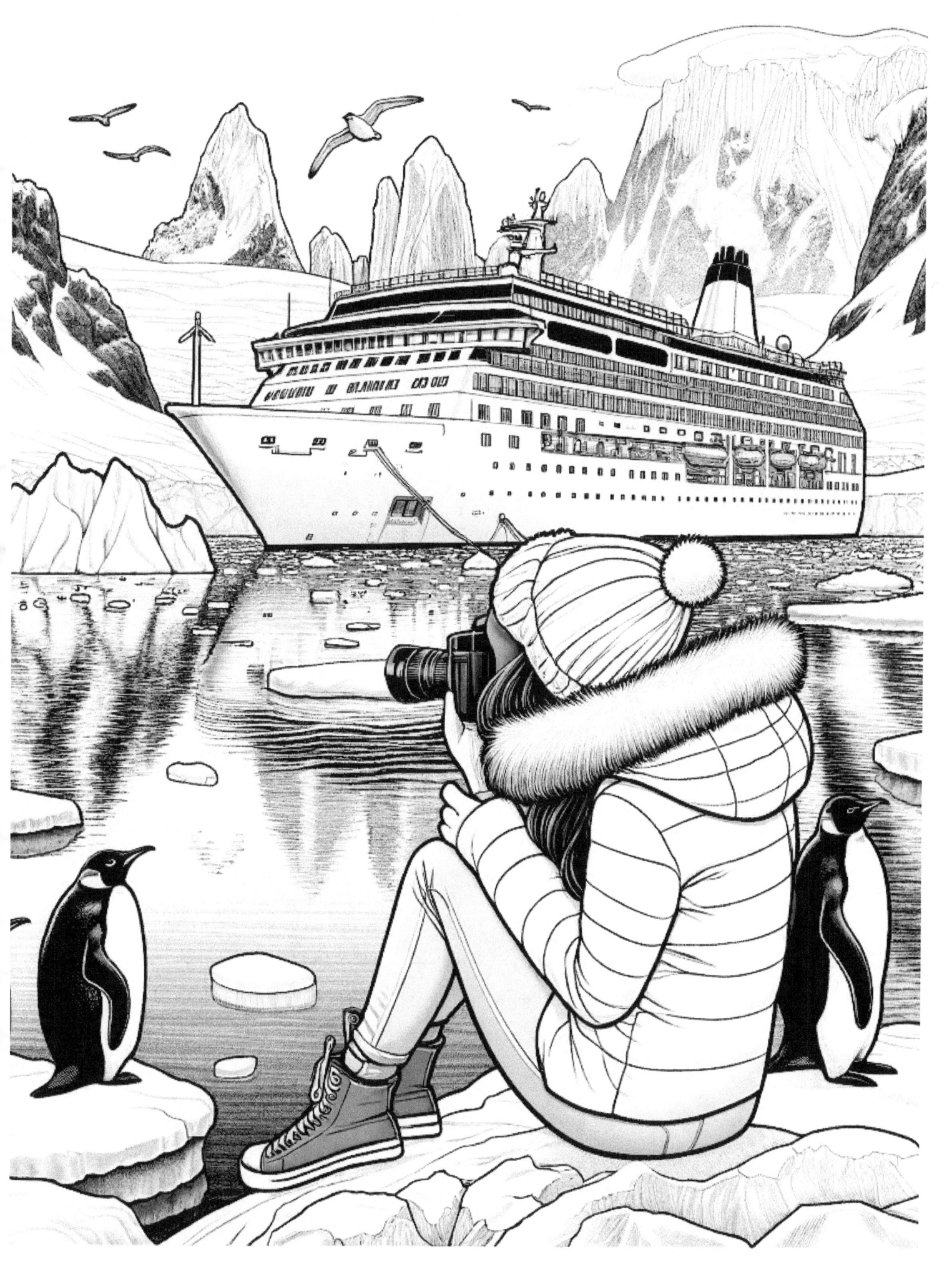

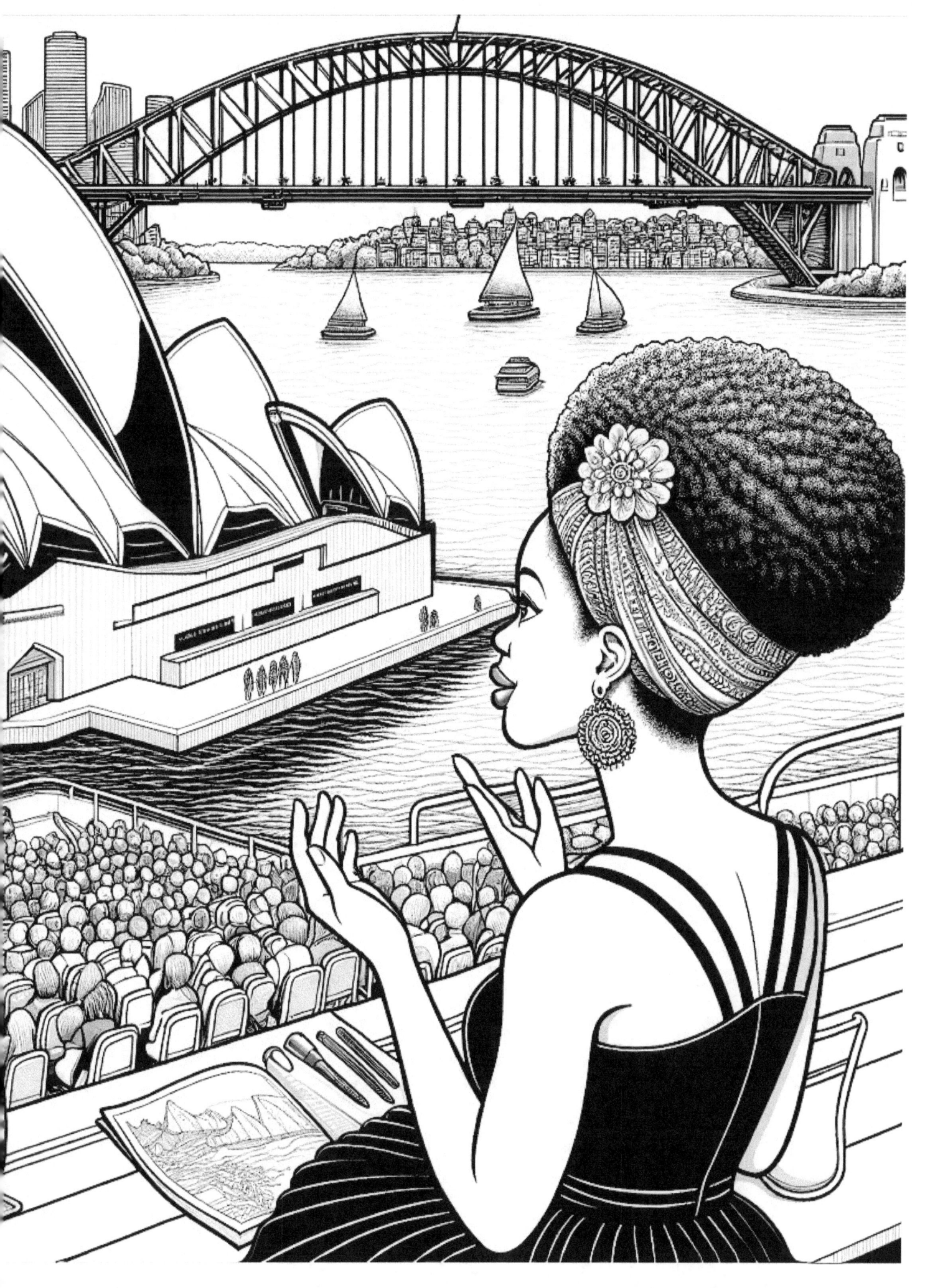

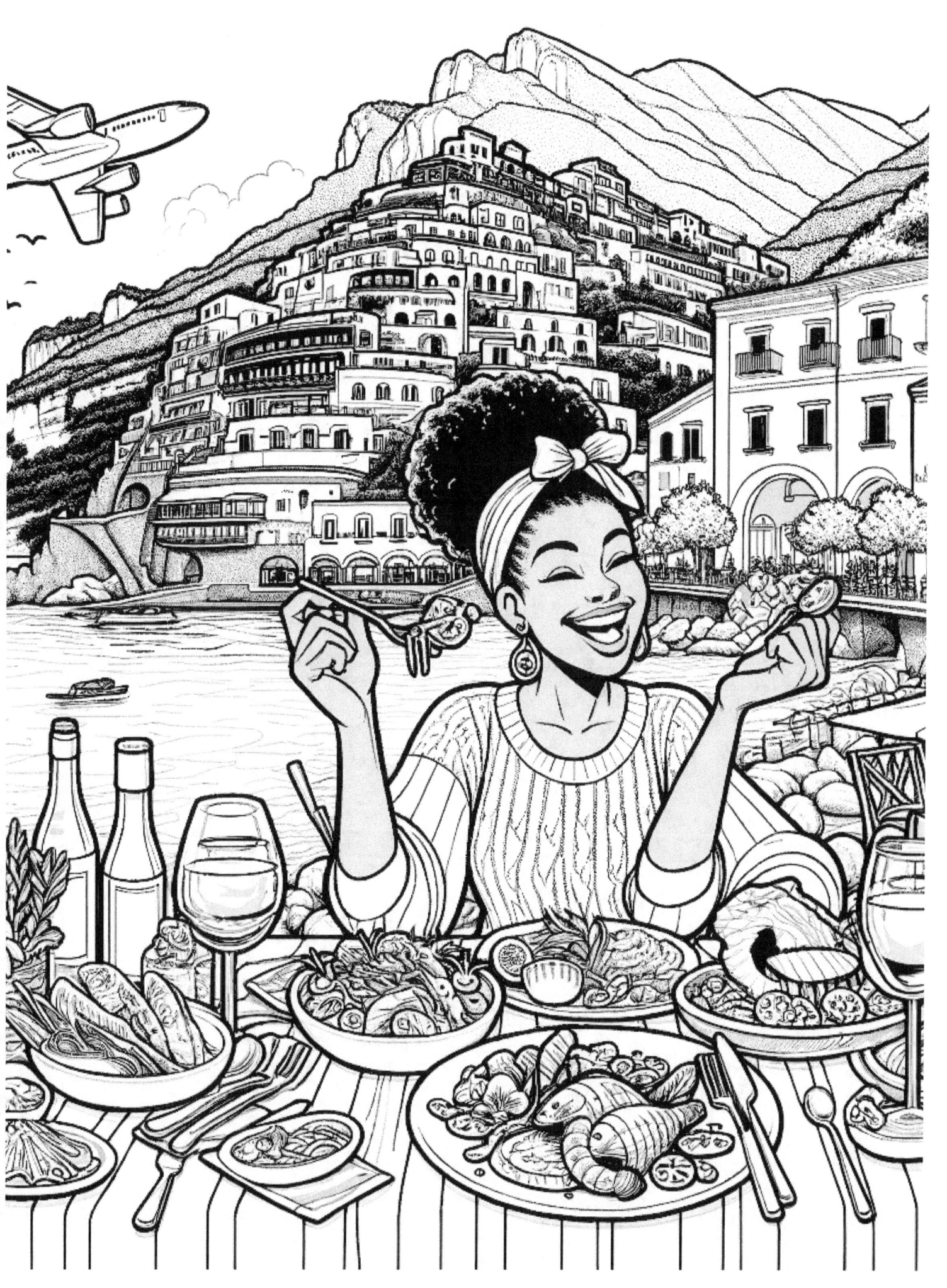

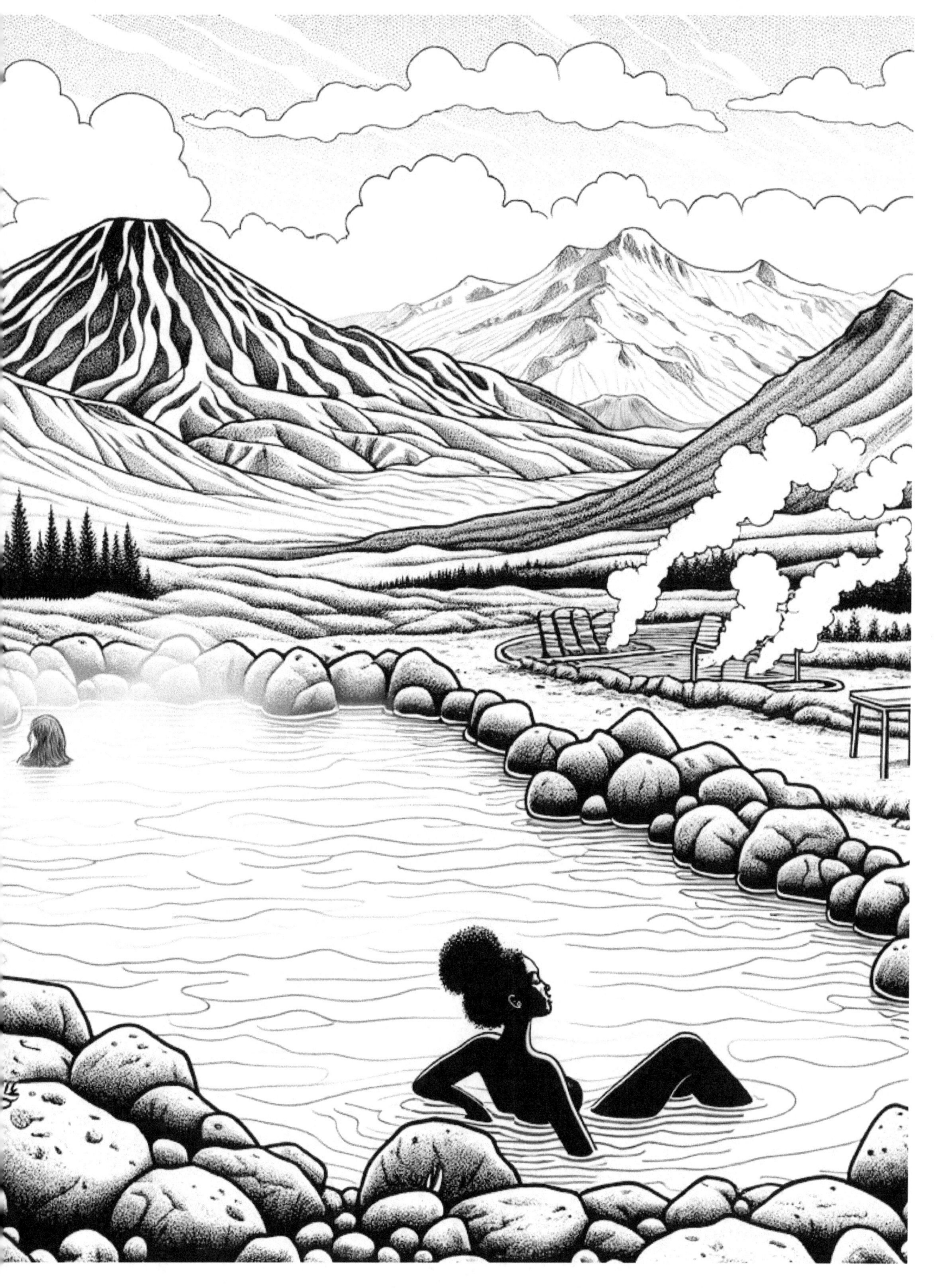

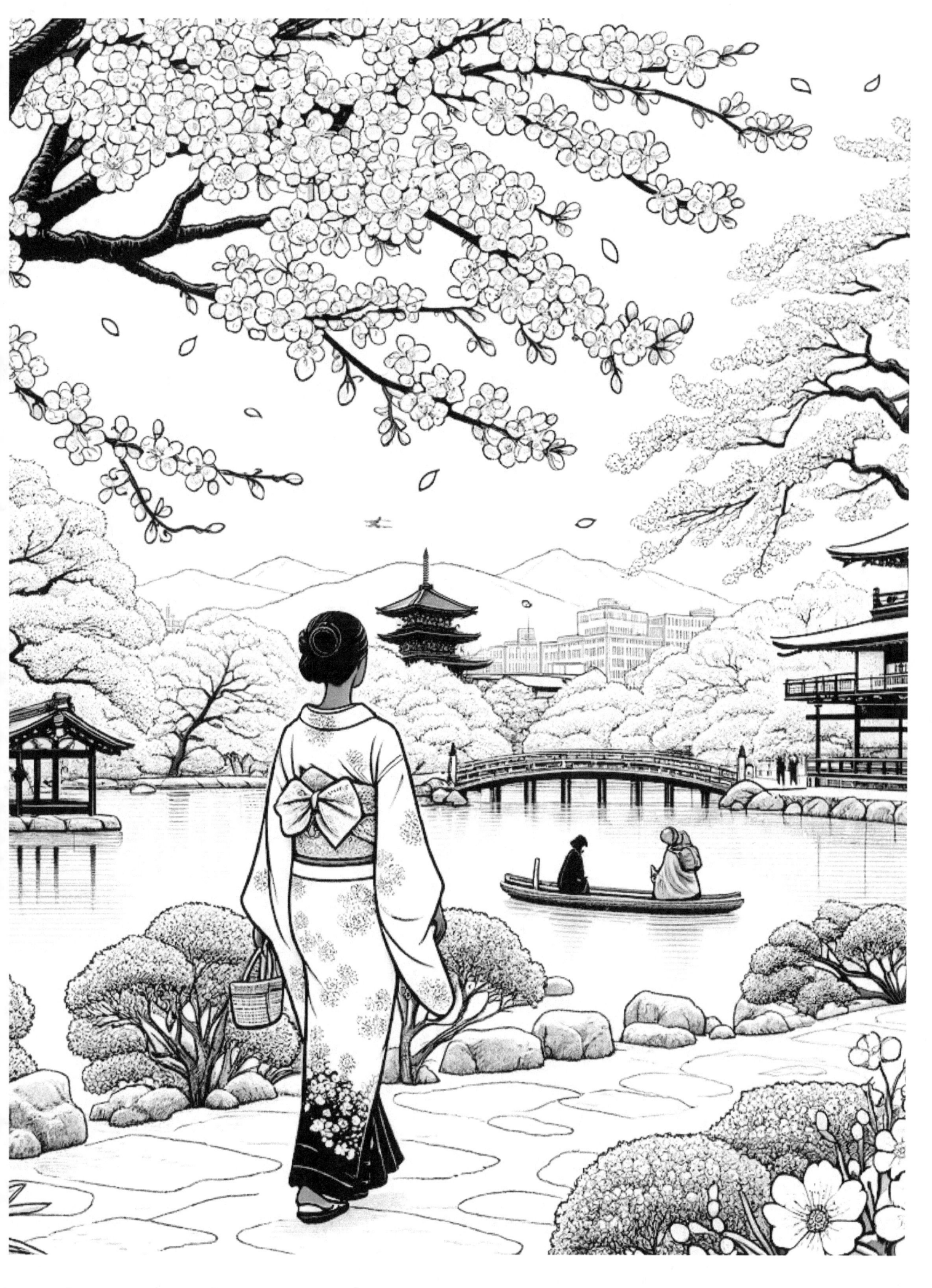

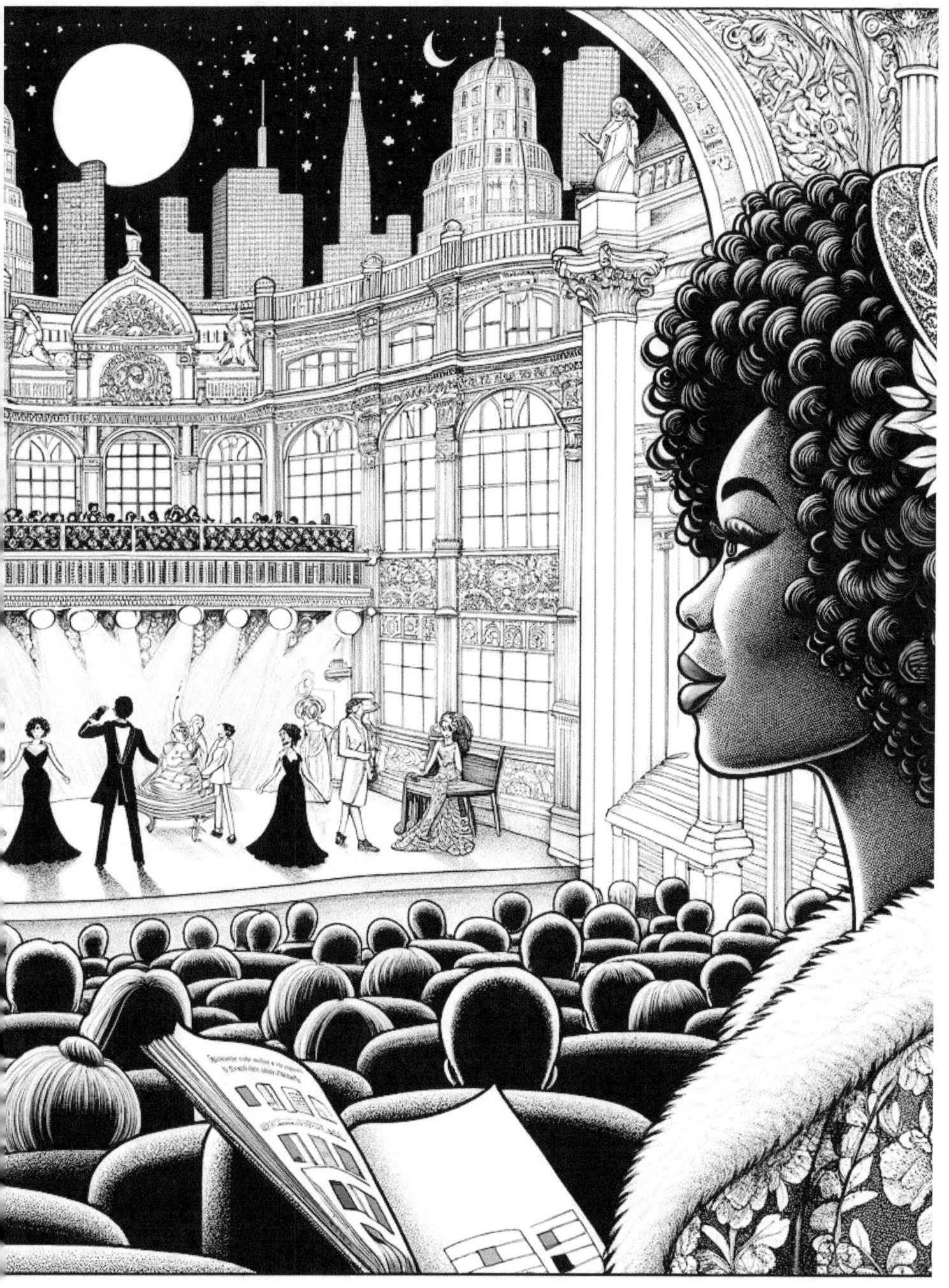

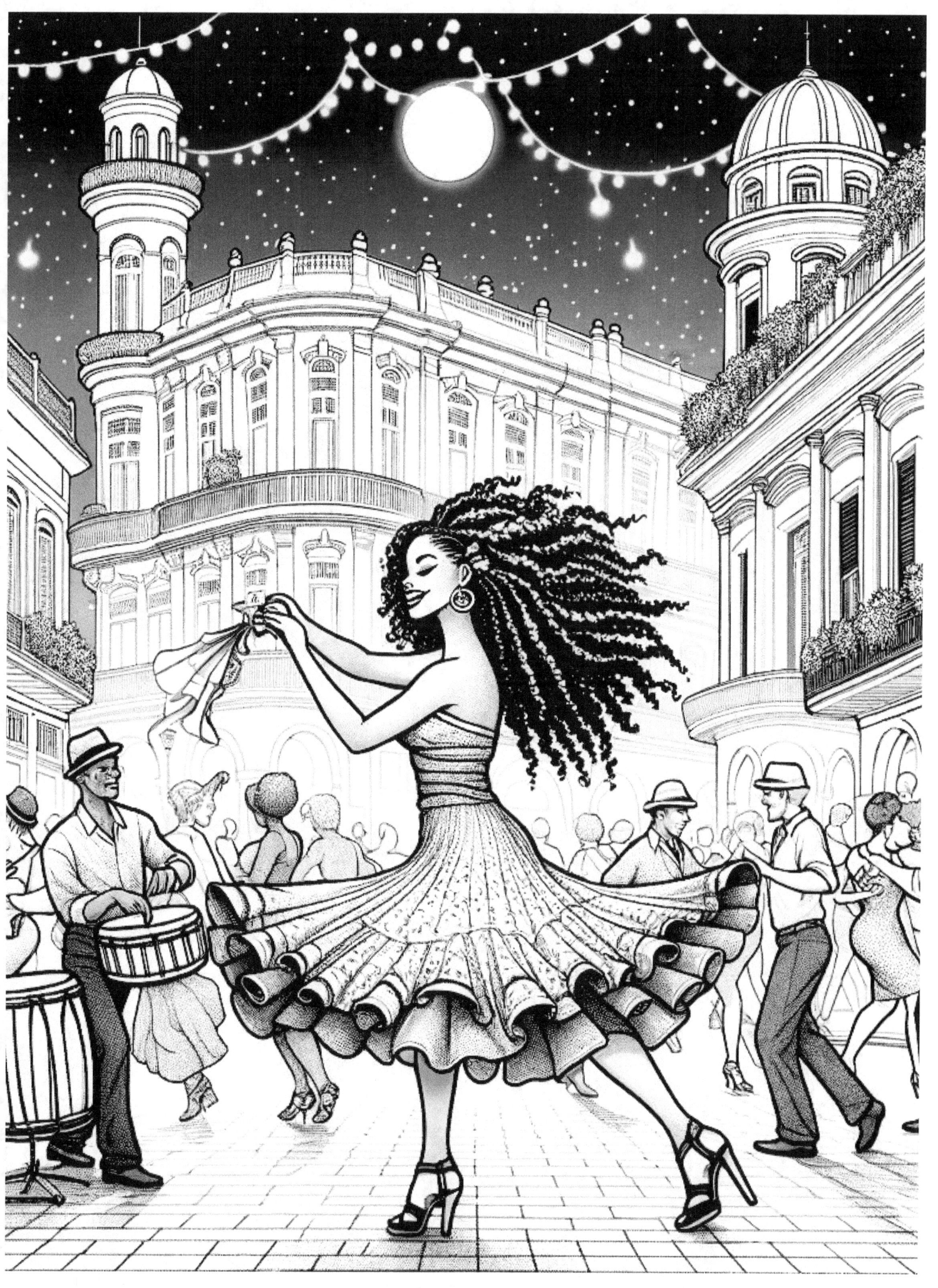

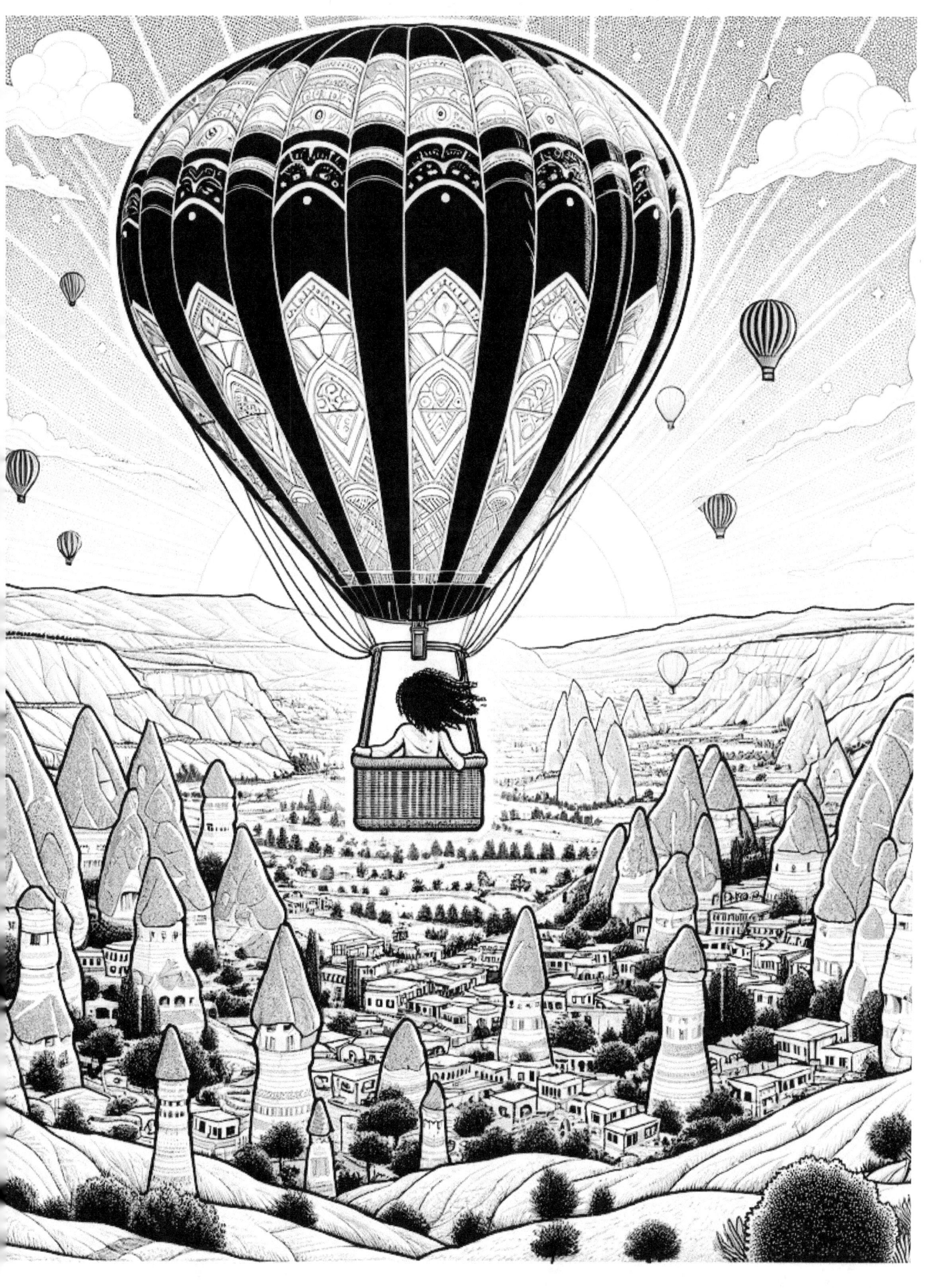

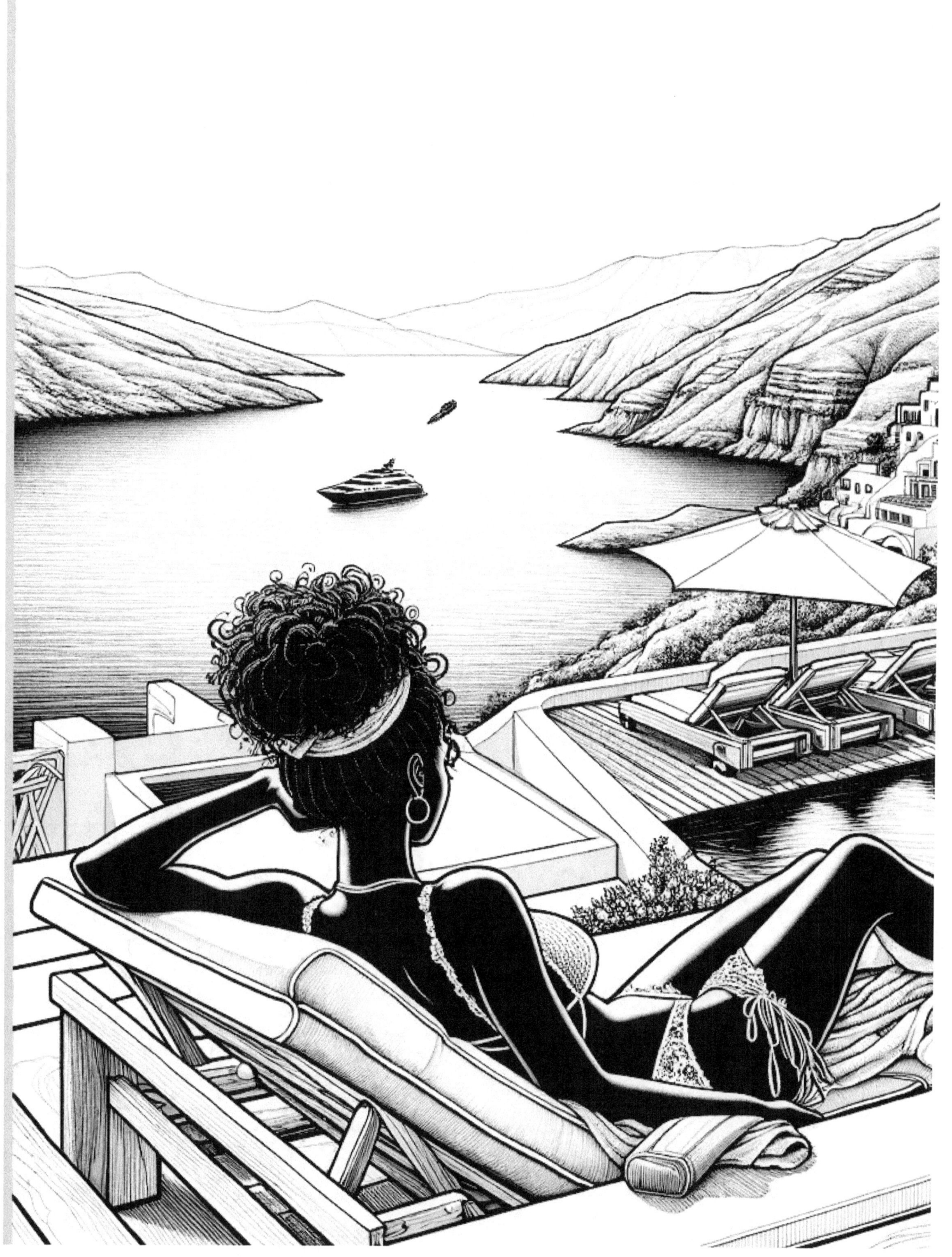

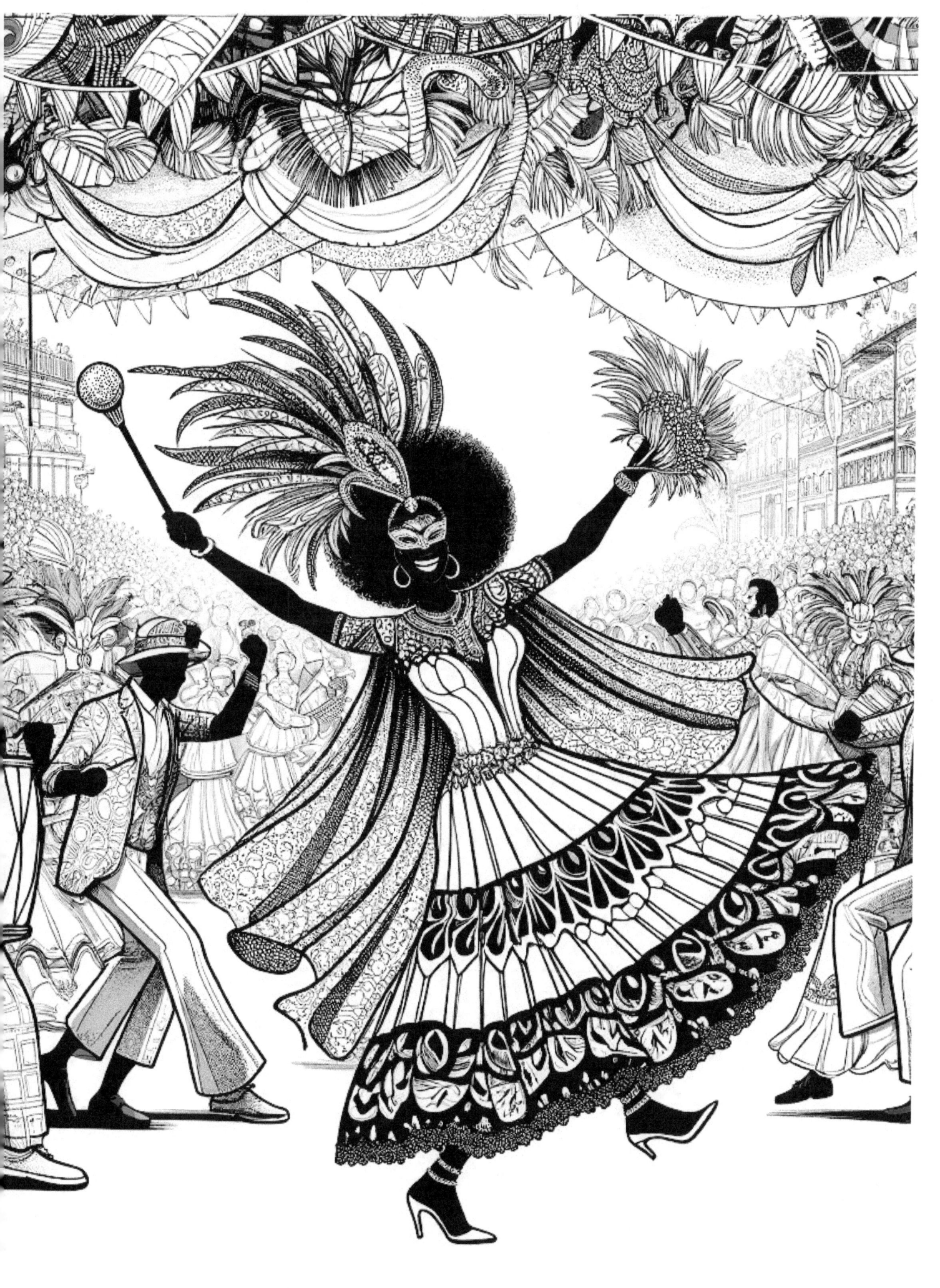

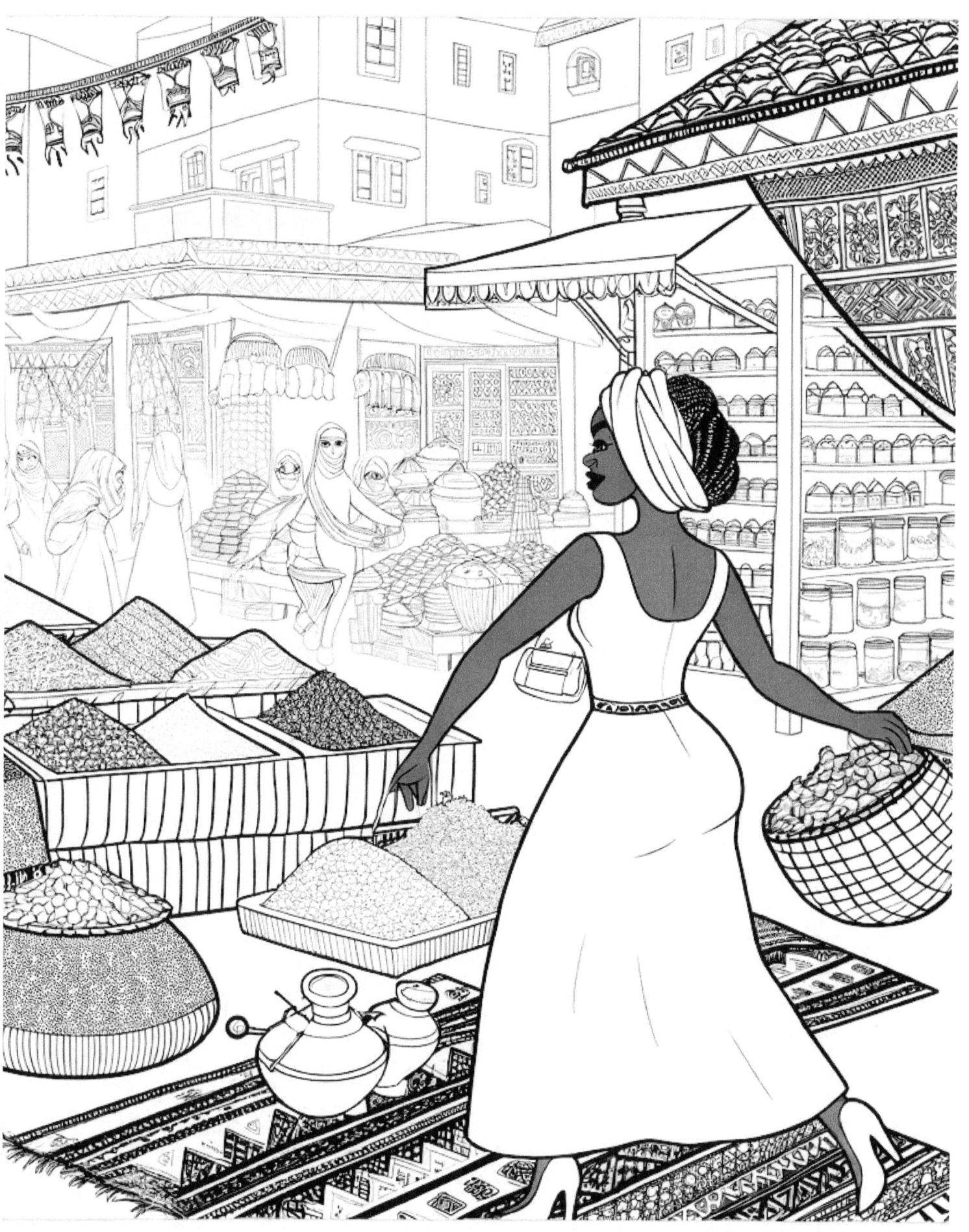

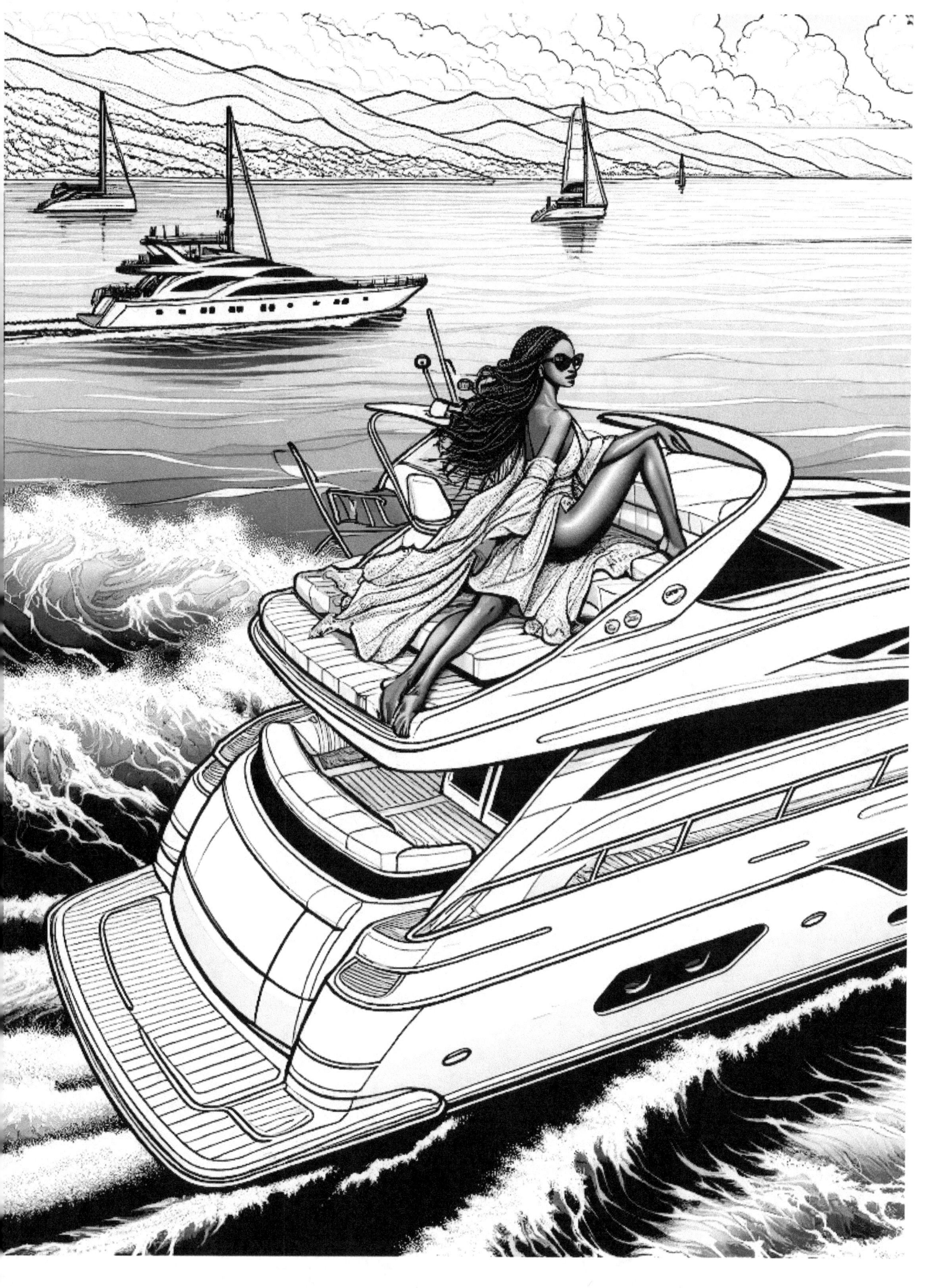

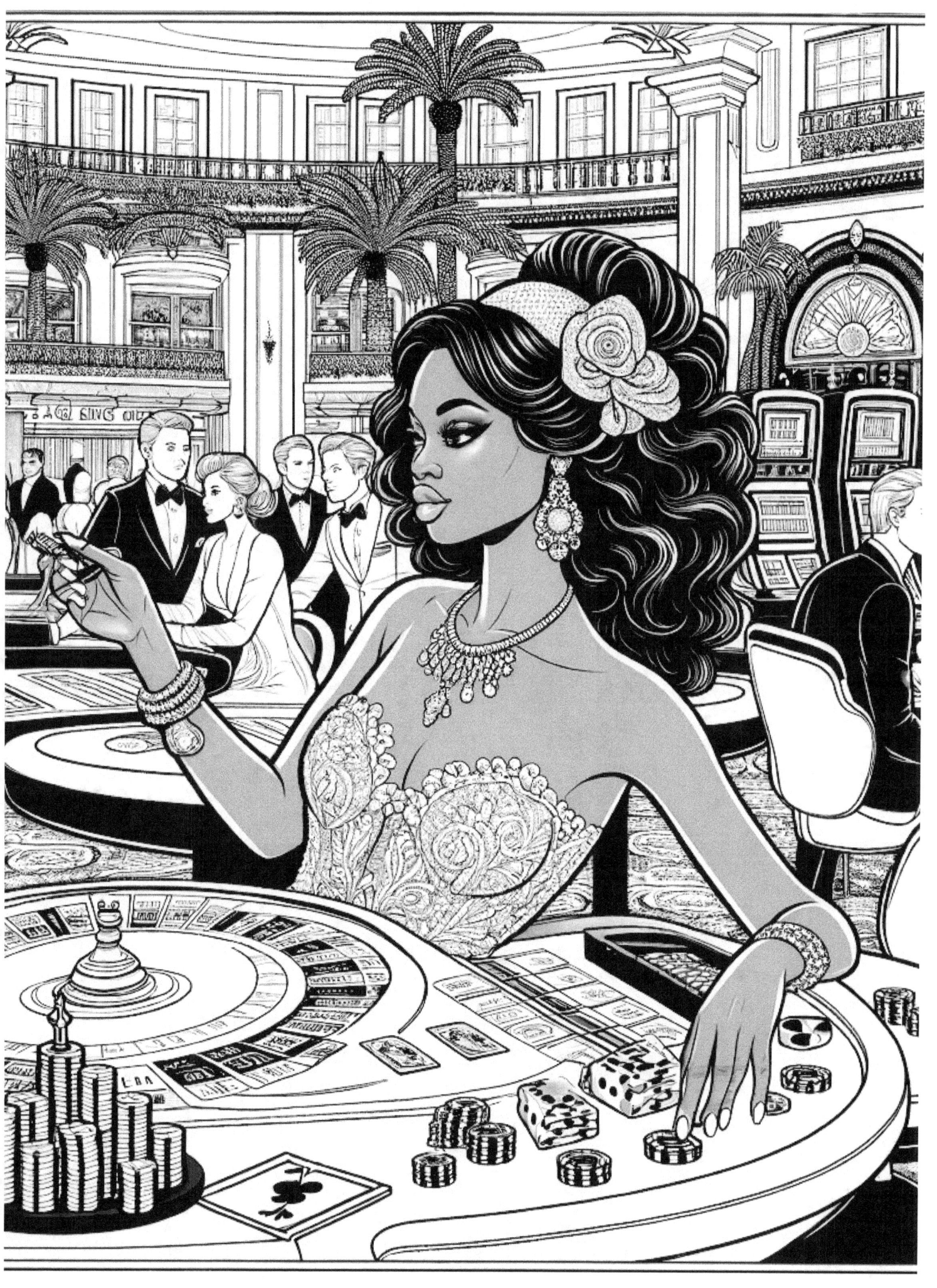

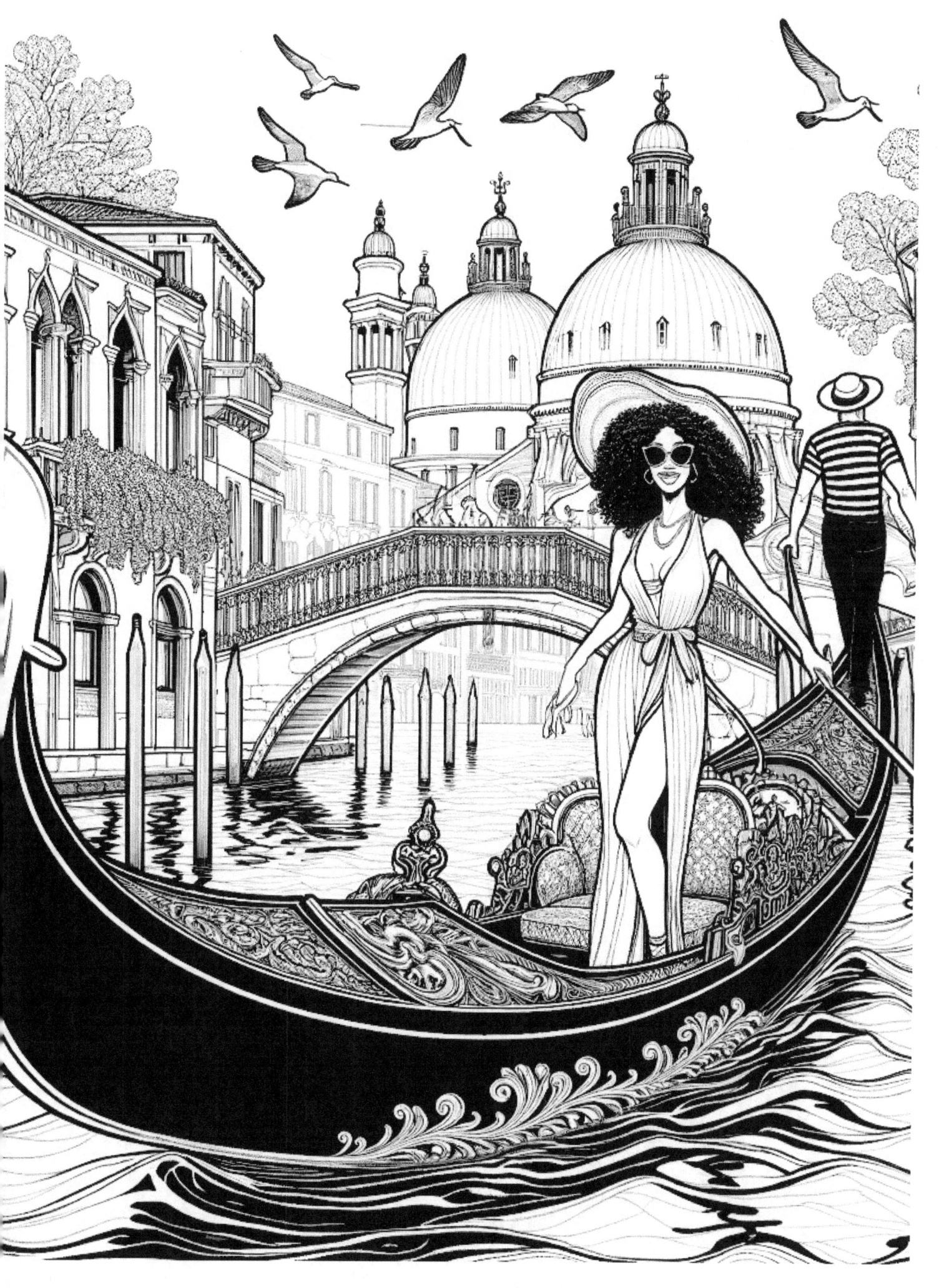

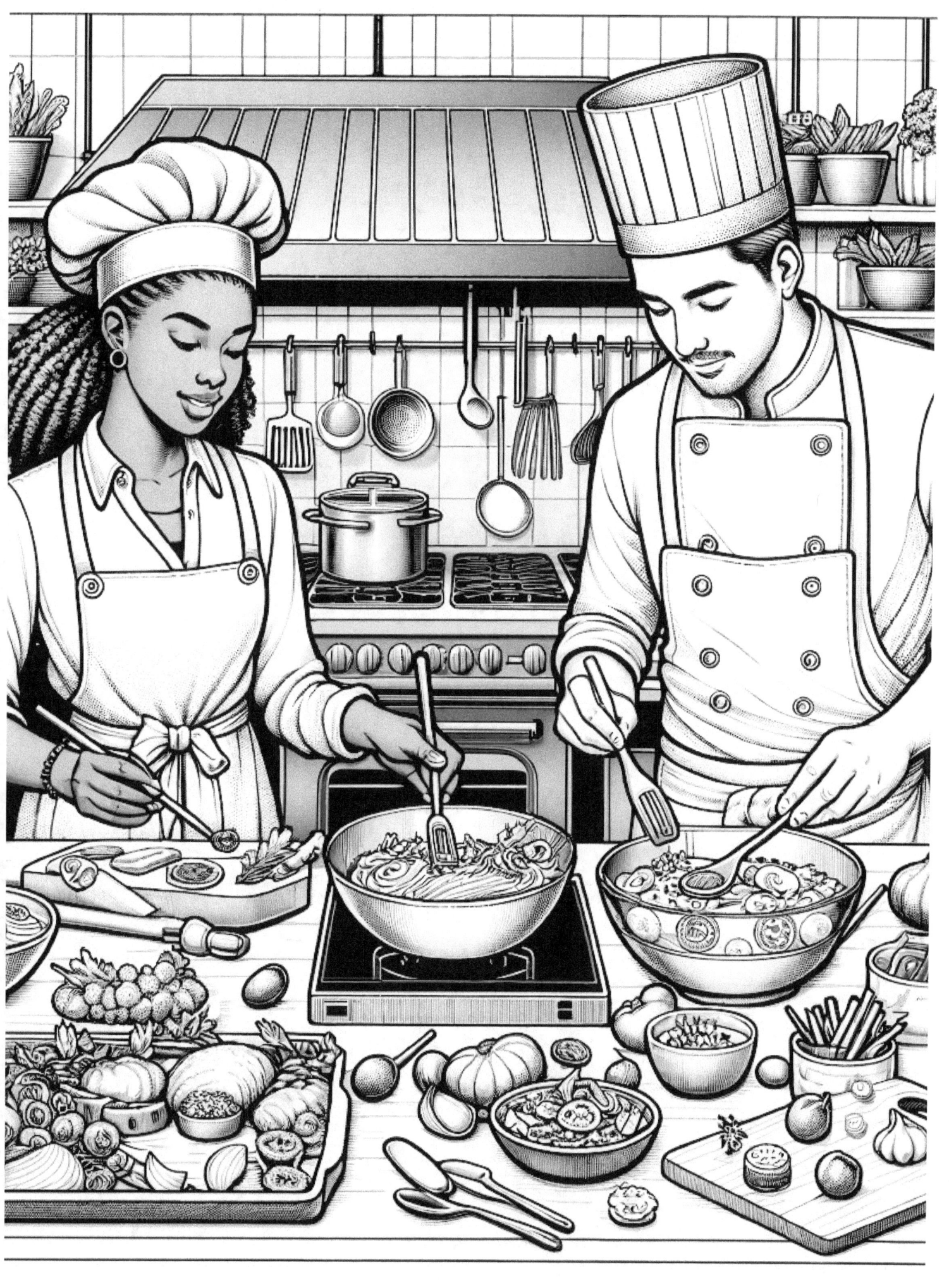

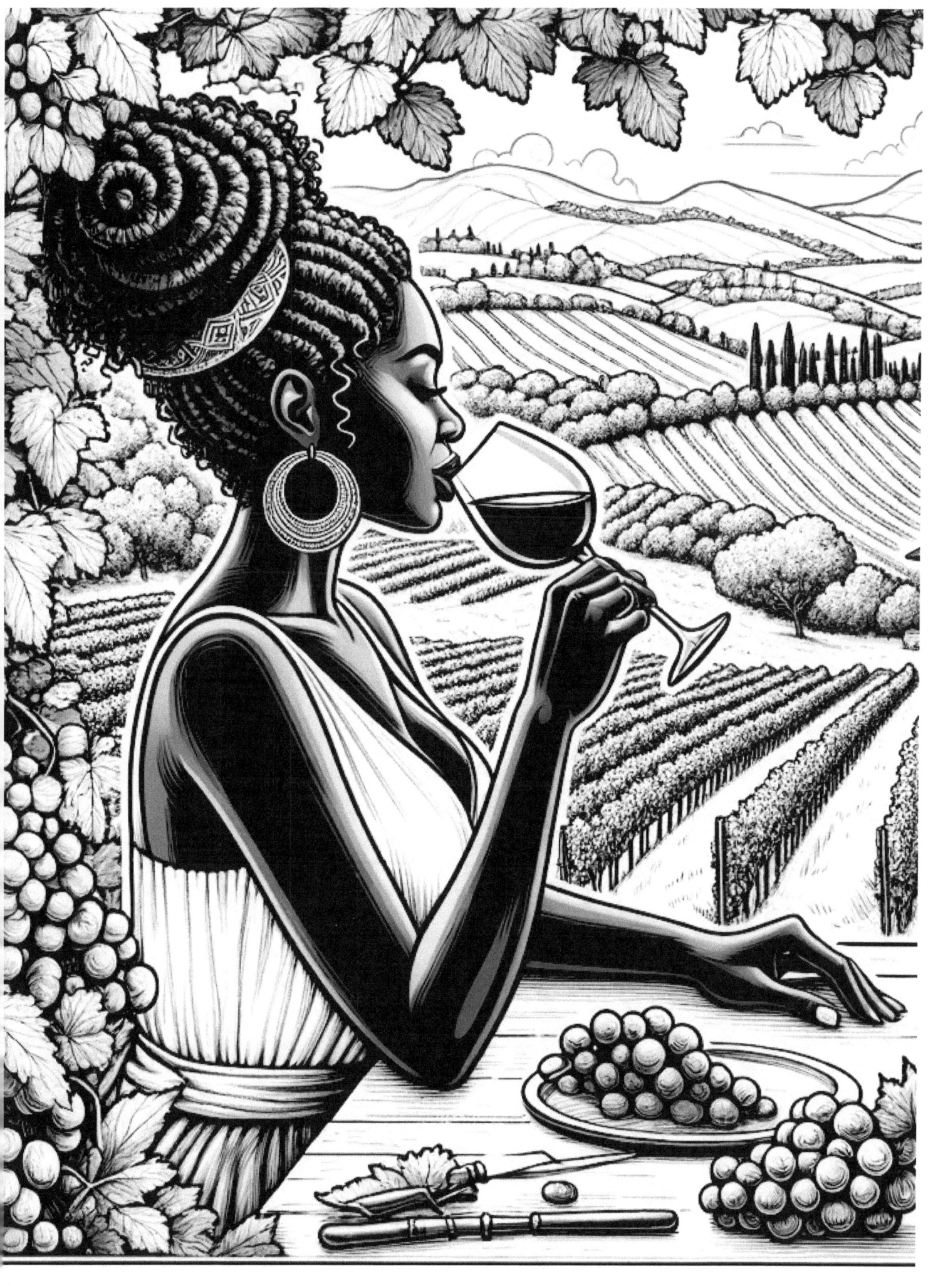

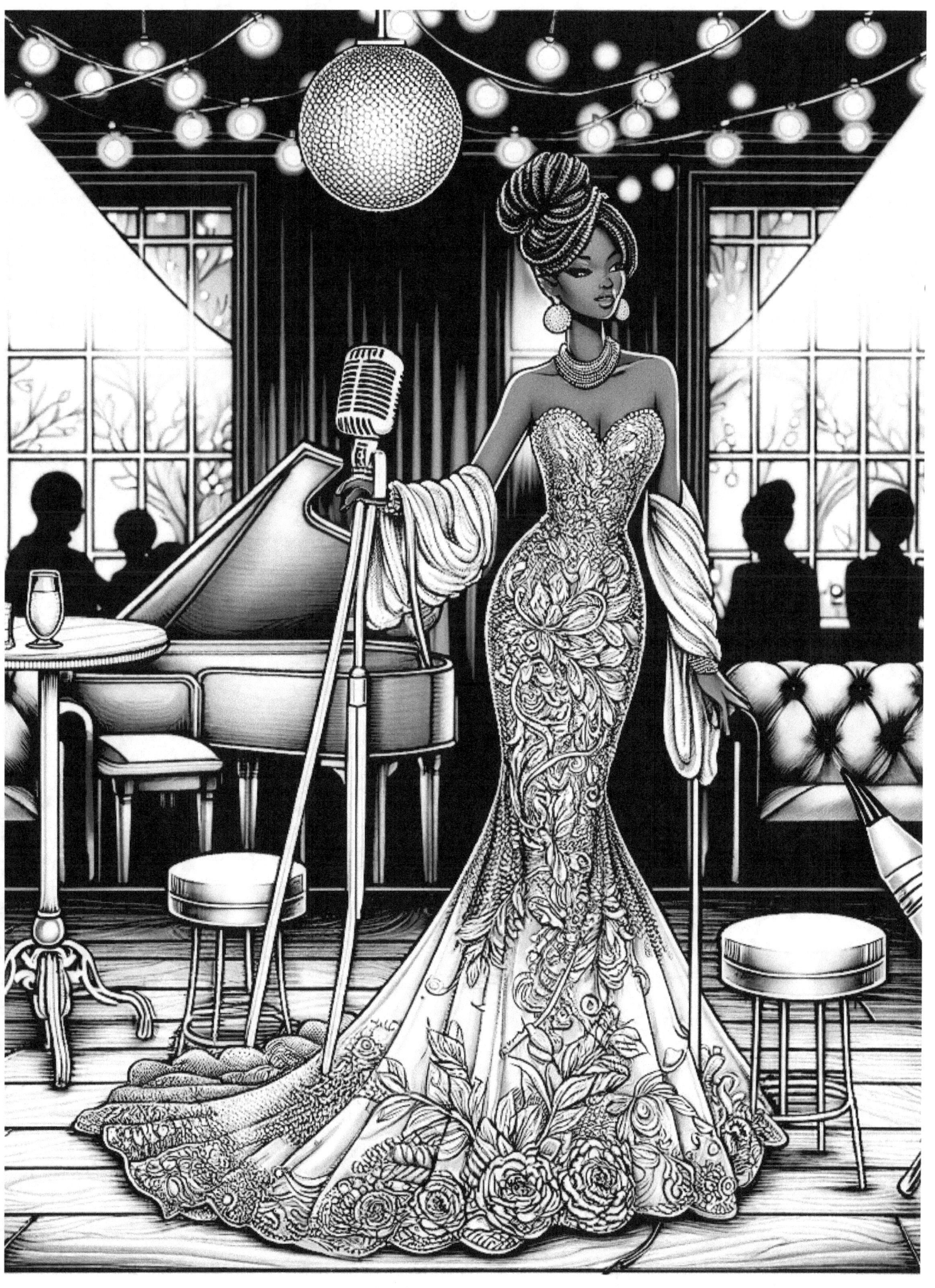

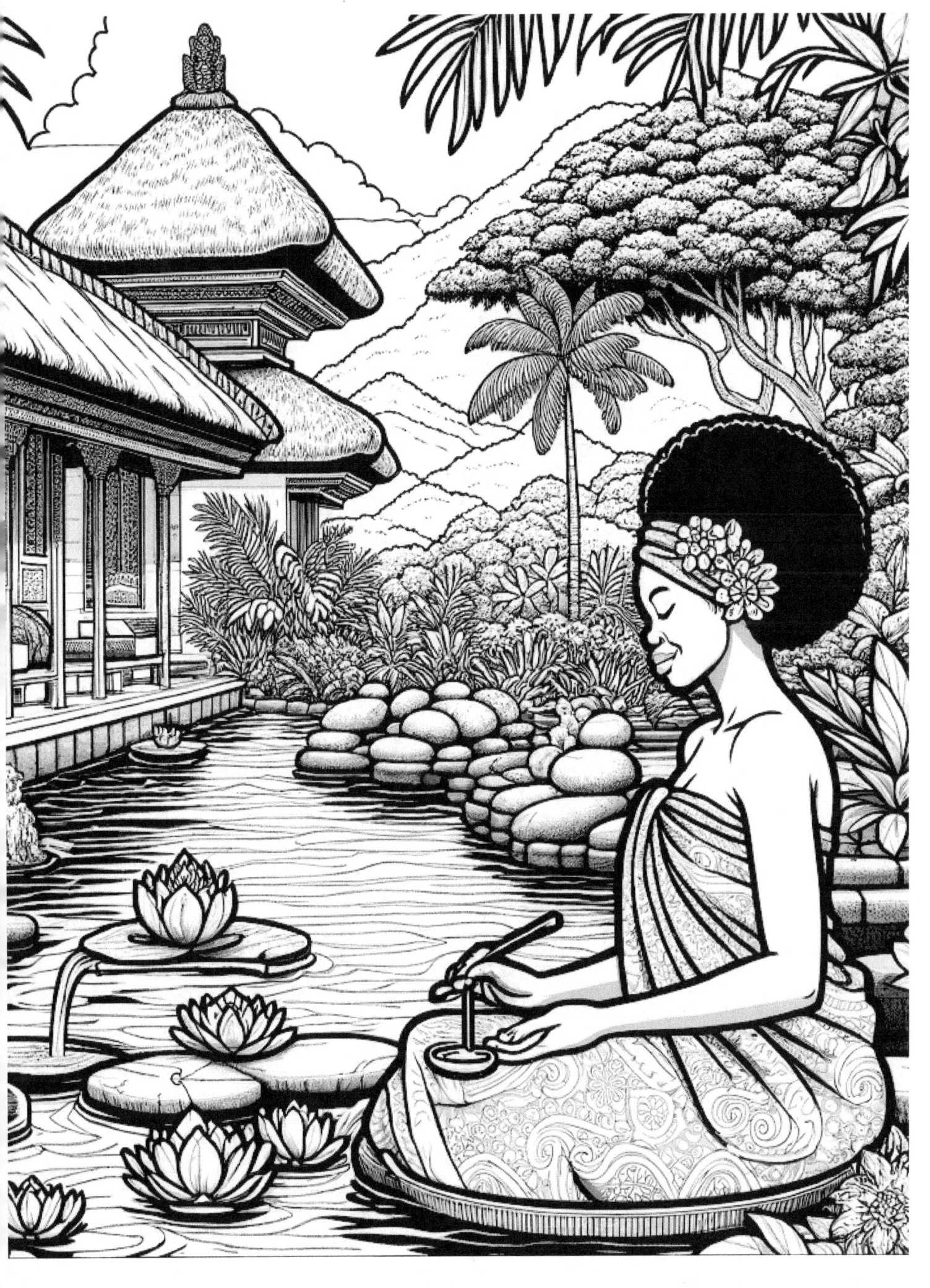

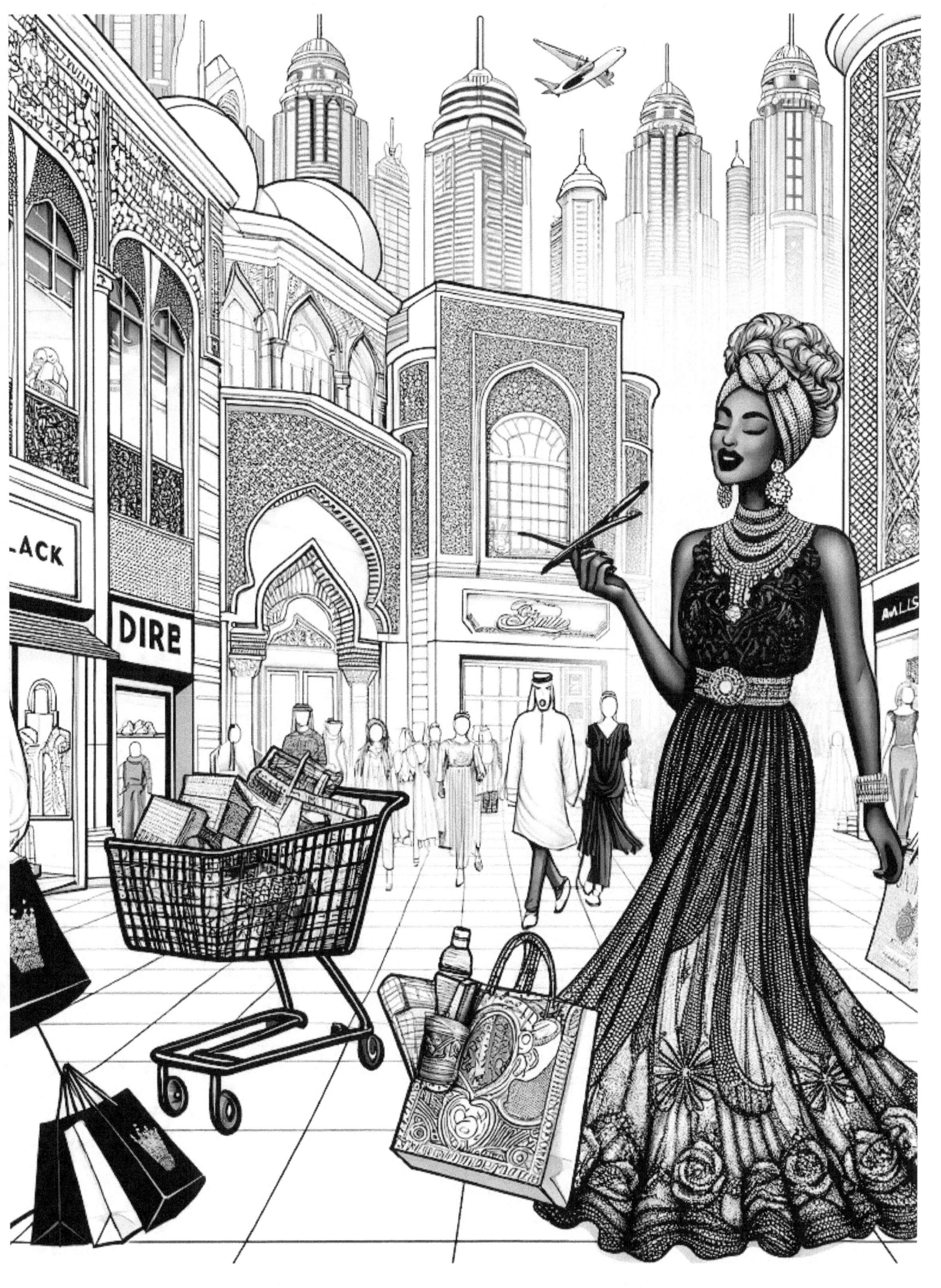

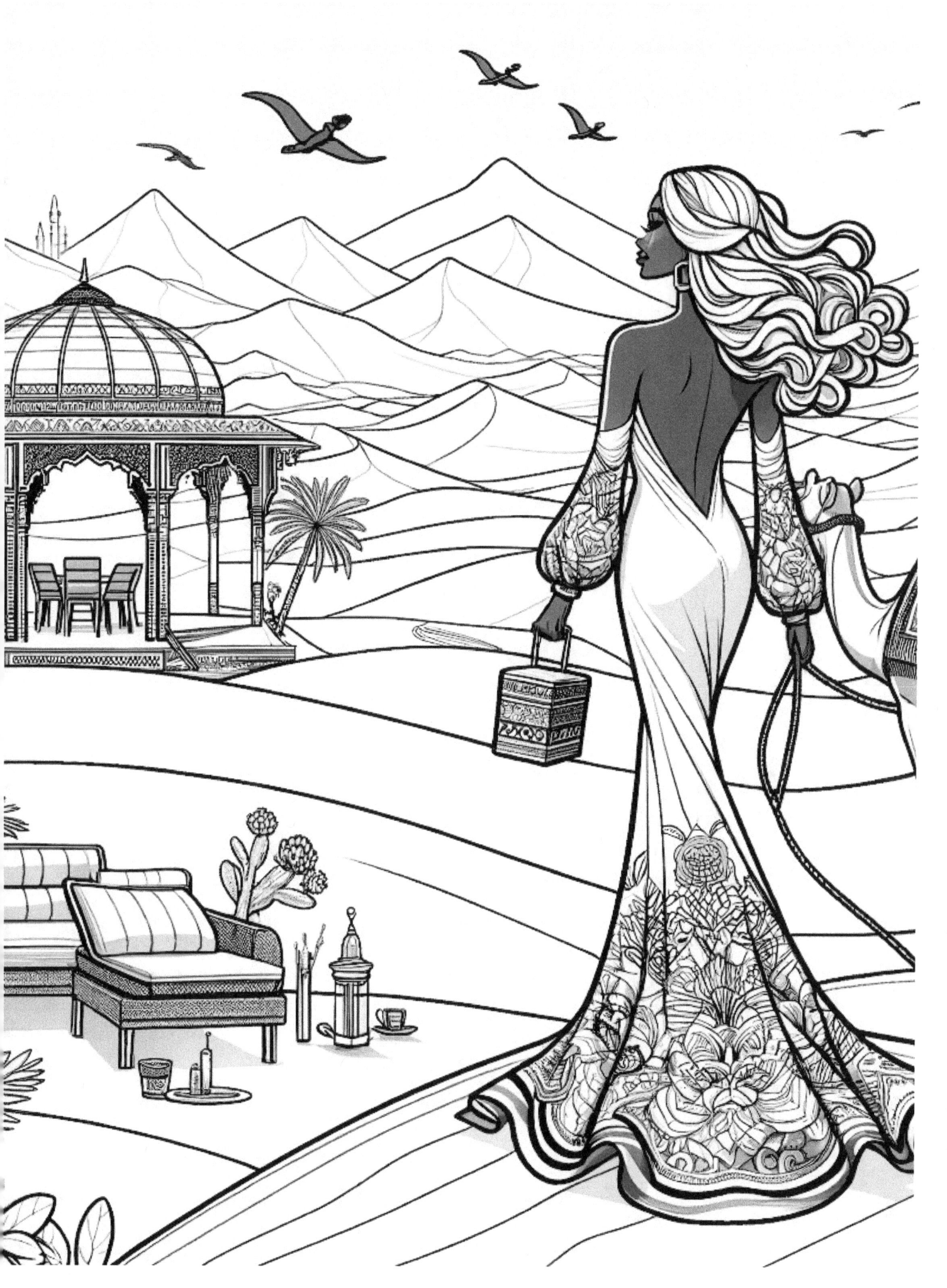

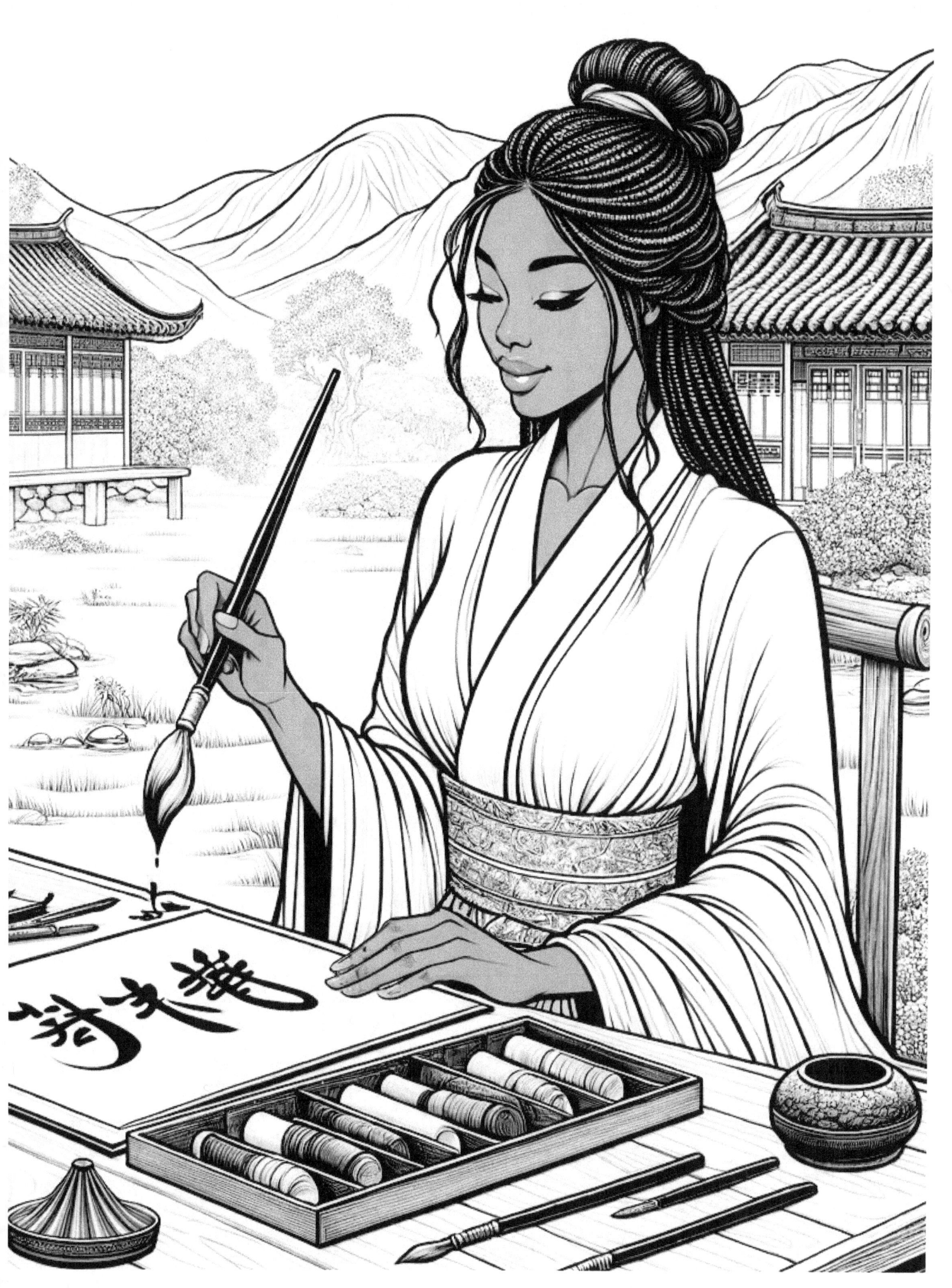

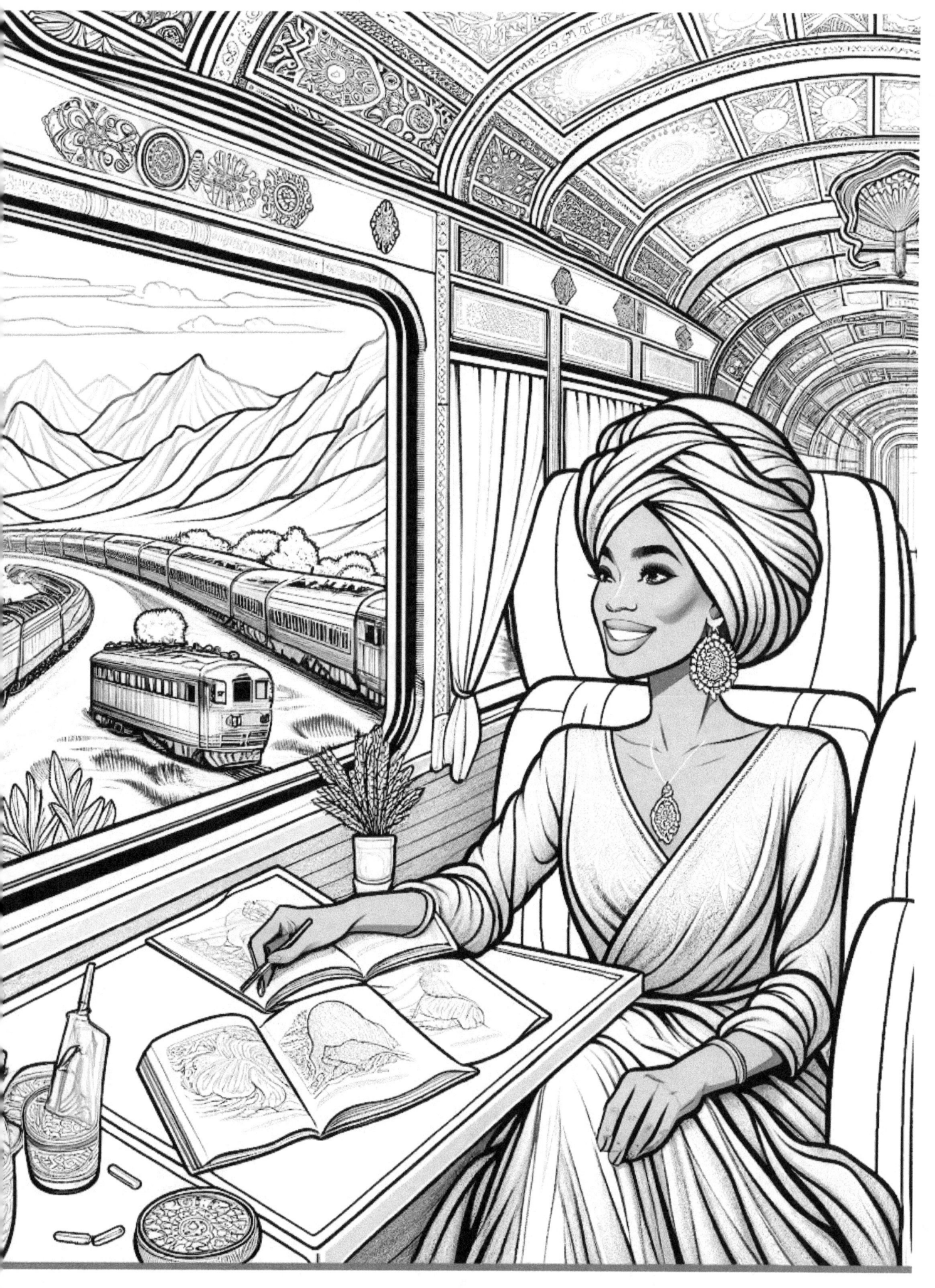

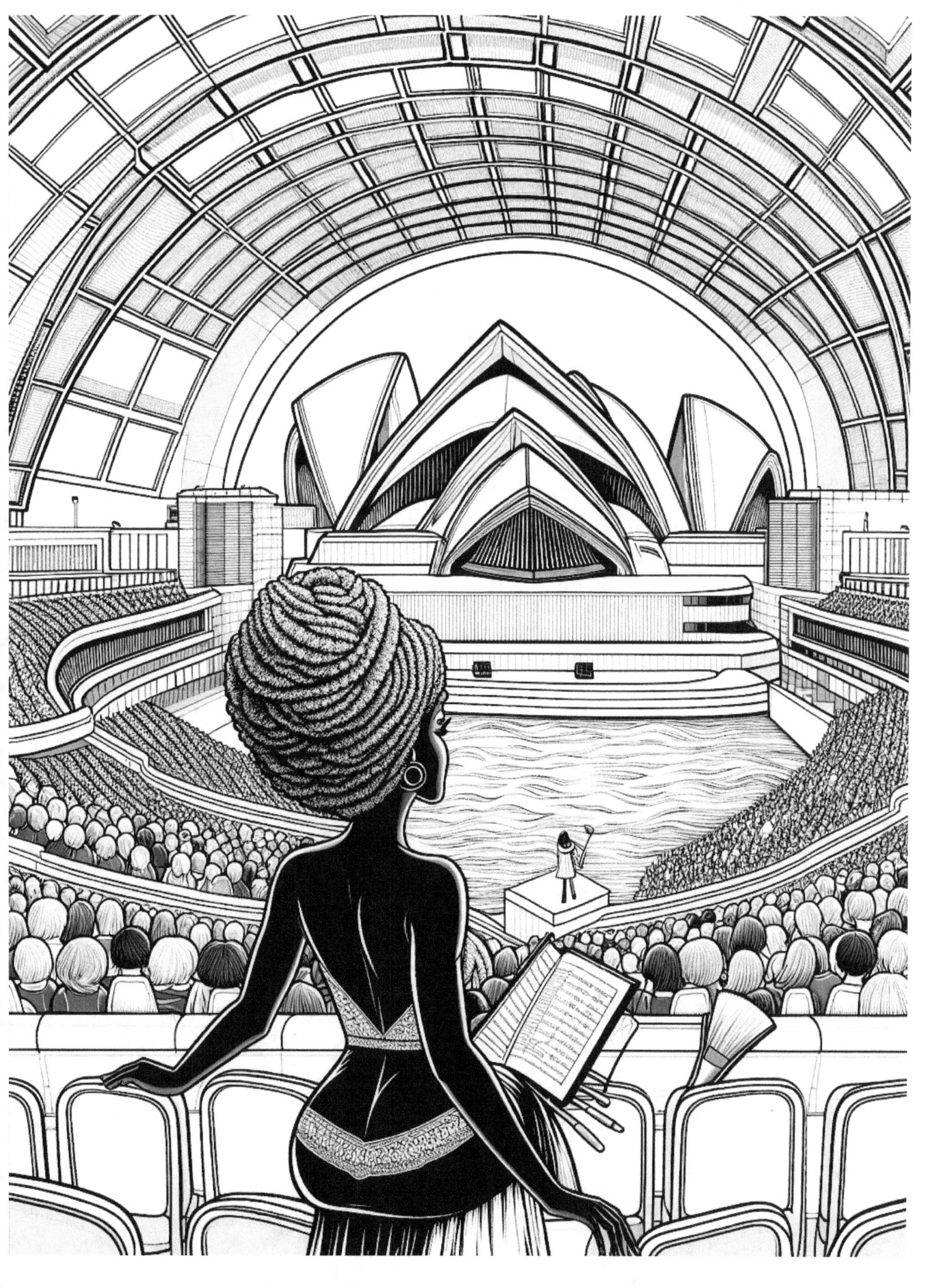

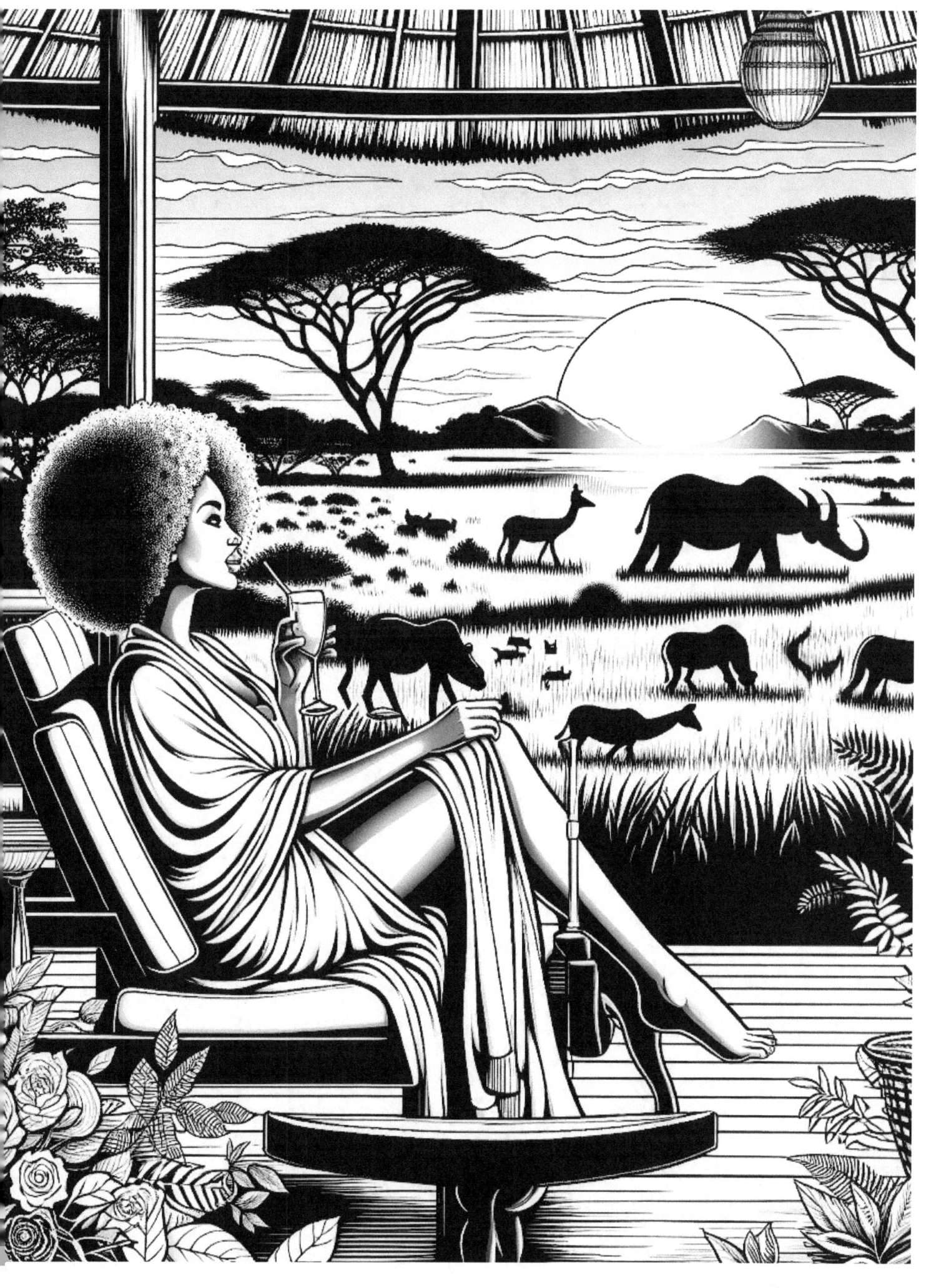

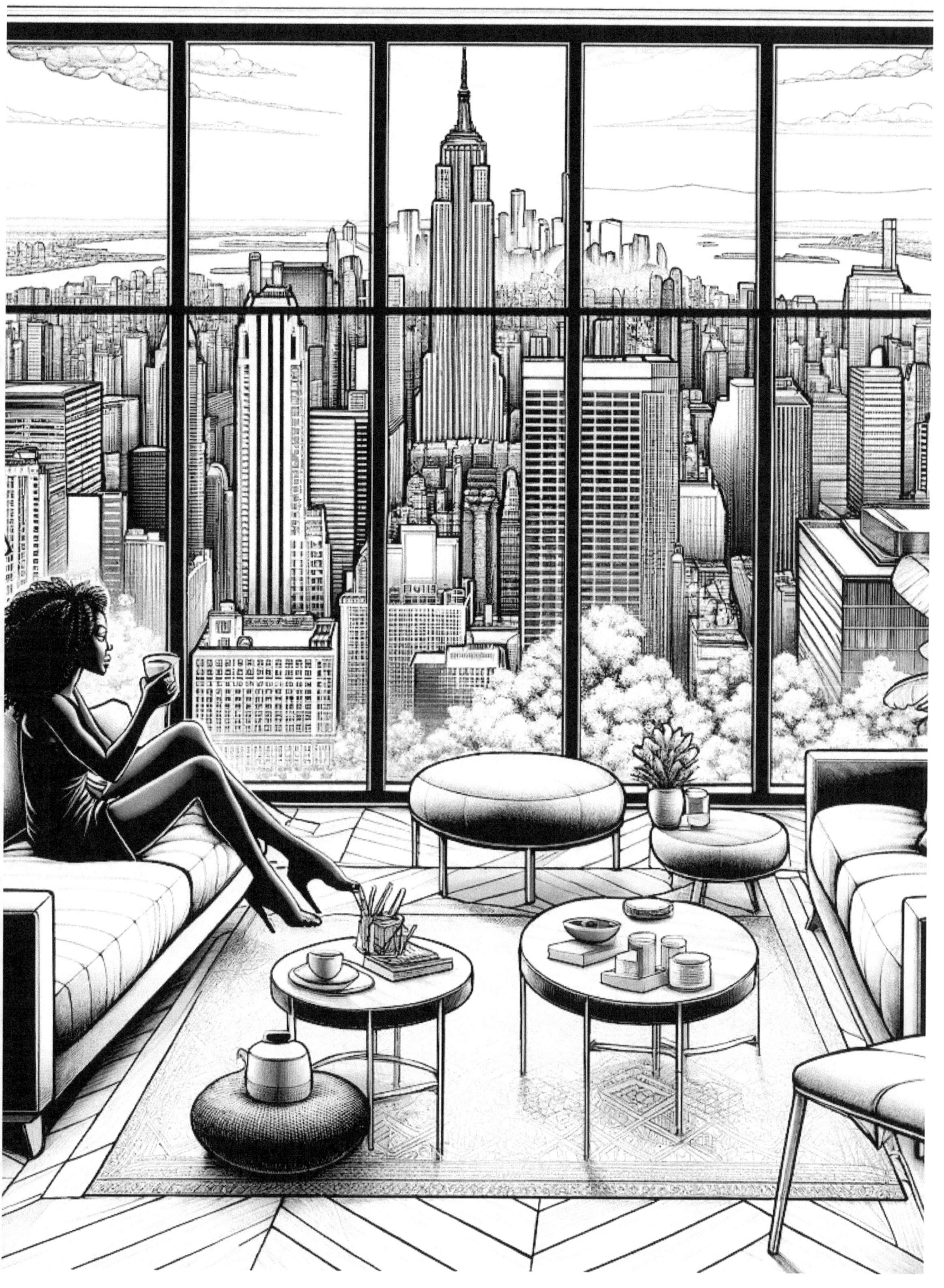